D1247013

The Yorkshire Terrier

OUR BEST FRIENDS

OUR BEST FRIENDS

The Yorkshire Terrier

Janice Biniok

636.7
BIN

ELDORADO INK

Produced by OTTN Publishing, Stockton, New Jersey

CADCC

Eldorado Ink
PO Box 100097
Pittsburgh, PA 15233
www.eldoradoink.com

Copyright © 2008 by Eldorado Ink. All rights reserved.
Printed and bound in Malaysia.

First printing

1 3 5 7 9 8 6 4 2

Library of Congress Cataloging-in-Publication Data

Biniok, Janice.
  The Yorkshire terrier / Janice Biniok.
      p. cm. — (Our best friends)
  Includes bibliographical references and index.
  ISBN-13: 978-1-932904-26-0 (hc)
  ISBN-10: 1-932904-26-3 (hc)
  1. Yorkshire terrier. I. Title.
  SF429.Y6B56 2008
  636.76—dc22

                        2007044880

Photo credits: © American Animal Hospital Association: 68;
© iStockphoto.com/Vicente Barcelo Varona: 85; © iStockphoto.com/Anna
Bryukhanova: 108; © iStockphoto.com/Dan Eckert: 66; © iStockphoto.com/Dennis
Guyitt: 92; © iStockphoto.com/Justin Horrocks: 110; © iStockphoto.com/Britta
Kasholm-Tengve: 28; © iStockphoto.com/Leslie Morris: 90; © iStockphoto.com/
Joey Nelson: 103; © iStockphoto.com/Brian Pamphilon: 3; © iStockphoto.com/
Lynn Paukovitch: 59; © iStockphoto.com/Achim Prill: 50; © 2008 Jupiterimages
Corporation: 8, 18, 76; © National Geographic/Getty Images: 98; Used under
license from Shutterstock, Inc.: 11, 12, 16 (all), 19, 21, 25, 27, 29, 32, 33, 34, 36,
37, 38, 42, 45, 48, 49, 54, 56, 58, 61, 62, 64, 67, 70 (all), 72 (all), 74, 78, 80, 81,
82, 86, 87, 89, 94, 97, 100, 102, 107, front cover (all), back cover.

TABLE OF CONTENTS

Introduction

GARY KORSGAARD, DVM

The mutually beneficial relationship between humans and animals began long before the dawn of recorded history. Archaeologists believe that humans began to capture and tame wild goats, sheep, and pigs more than 9,000 years ago. These animals were then bred for specific purposes, such as providing humans with a reliable source of food or providing furs and hides that could be used for clothing or the construction of dwellings.

Other animals had been sought for companionship and assistance even earlier. The dog, believed to be the first animal domesticated, began living and working with Stone Age humans in Europe more than 14,000 years ago. Some archaeologists believe that wild dogs and humans were drawn together because both hunted the same prey. By taming and training dogs, humans became more effective hunters. Dogs, meanwhile, enjoyed the social contact with humans and benefited from greater access to food and warm shelter. Dogs soon became beloved pets as

well as trusted workers. This can be seen from the many artifacts depicting dogs that have been found at ancient sites in Asia, Europe, North America, and the Middle East.

The earliest domestic cats appeared in the Middle East about 5,000 years ago. Small wild cats were probably first attracted to human settlements because plenty of rodents could be found wherever harvested grain was stored. Cats played a useful role in hunting and killing these pests, and it is likely that grateful humans rewarded them for this assistance. Over time, these small cats gave up some of their aggressive wild behaviors and began living among humans. Cats eventually became so popular in ancient Egypt that they were believed to possess magical powers. Cat statues were placed outside homes to ward off evil spirits, and mummified cats were included in royal tombs to accompany their owners into the afterlife.

Today, few people believe that cats have supernatural powers, but most pet owners feel a magical bond with their pets, whether they are dogs, cats, hamsters, rabbits, horses, or parrots. The lives of pets and their people become inextricably intertwined, providing strong emotional and physical rewards for both humans and animals. People of all ages can benefit from the loving companionship of a pet. Not surprisingly, then, pet ownership is widespread. Recent statistics indicate that about 60 percent of all households in the United States and Canada have at least one pet, while the figure is close to 50 percent of households in the United Kingdom. For millions of people, therefore, pets truly have become their "best friends."

Finding the best animal friend can be a challenge, however. Not only are there many types of domesticated pets, but each has specific needs, characteristics, and personality traits. Even within a category of pets, such as dogs, different breeds will flourish in different surroundings and with different treatment. For example, a German Shepherd may not be the right pet for a person living in a cramped urban apartment; that person might be better off caring for a smaller dog like a Toy Poodle or Shih Tzu, or perhaps a cat. On the other hand, an active person who loves the outdoors may prefer the companion-

ship of a Labrador Retriever to that of a small dog or a passive indoor pet like a goldfish or hamster.

The joys of pet ownership come with certain responsibilities. Bringing a pet into your home and your neighborhood obligates you to care for and train the pet properly. For example, a dog must be housebroken, taught to obey your commands, and trained to behave appropriately when he encounters other people or animals. Owners must also be mindful of their pet's particular nutritional and medical needs.

The purpose of the OUR BEST FRIENDS series is to provide a helpful and comprehensive introduction to pet ownership. Each book contains the basic information a prospective pet owner needs in order to choose the right pet for his or her situation and to care for that pet throughout the pet's lifetime. Training, socialization, proper nutrition, potential medical issues, and the legal responsibilities of pet ownership are thoroughly explained and discussed, and an abundance of expert tips and suggestions are offered. Whether it is a hamster, corn snake, guinea pig, or Labrador Retriever, the books in the OUR BEST FRIENDS series provide everything the reader needs to know about how to have a happy, well-adjusted, and well-behaved pet.

CHAPTER ONE

Is a Yorkshire Terrier Right for You?

The adorable Yorkshire Terrier, with his full, flowing tresses, makes an elegant and impressive lapdog. But beneath the Yorkie's petite and primped exterior lies the heart of a tiger. Although he's considered among the elite of canine arm candy, the Yorkie has not forgotten his working-class heritage as a ratter during the Industrial Revolution in England. His body has since become smaller, but his courage has remained intact.

Is this feisty little terrier the ideal companion for you? Certainly, there are many advantages to the Yorkie's tiny size and "big dog" personality, but these characteristics also present challenges that a potential owner should consider. A closer look at the Yorkie's physical and temperamental characteristics will help you decide if a Yorkie should be in your future.

PHYSICAL CHARACTERISTICS

If you were attracted to the Yorkie's stunning tan and blue coat and cute puppy face, you wouldn't be the first! He embodies the word *cute*. But his diminutive size affects the way he must be handled. To be a conscientious owner, you have to look beyond aesthetics.

Yorkies generally don't weigh more than seven pounds (3.2 kg). This makes them extremely portable. Perhaps you've seen celebrities carrying them around in their tote bags.

Such treatment exposes the dog to the danger of falls, however, so care should be taken. Being dropped from a human's arms could seriously injure a Yorkie. Owners must also be careful not to step on or accidentally kick the dog. With his small size, he gets underfoot easily, and the weight and force behind a human's movements could also be quite damaging.

The Yorkie's size isn't only a liability, though. Small dogs have many advantages. They are generally cheaper to care for because they consume considerably less food than a large dog would. They can also be kept in apartments and can be more easily exercised in small areas. For people planning to cuddle up with their little pooch, a small dog is also a lot less of a couch hog than a German Shepherd or a Labrador Retriever.

PERSONALITY TRAITS TO CONSIDER

The Yorkshire Terrier's temperament and physical characteristics appear to be at odds with each other, but they actually complement each other beautifully. A small body with a big personality has proven to be a winning combination for this tenacious little dog.

INDEPENDENCE: The Yorkie's grit makes him a little less needy and a little more independent than other toy breeds. If you want a small dog that doesn't annoy you by constantly begging for attention, the Yorkie may be the dog of your dreams. This

YORKIE PERSONALITY PROFILE

Energy Level ....High to very high
Prey Drive ....High to very high
Intelligence/Trainability ....Moderate to high
Sociability..Moderate
Watchdog Capabilities ....Very high
Guard Dog Abilities ....Very Low
Dominance in Relation to Other Dogs ....Moderate to high

independence also makes the Yorkie one of the toy breeds that particularly appeals to men.

Because he has an independent attitude, the Yorkie is often viewed as stubborn and difficult to train. The truth is that independent-minded dogs can be trained just as easily as other dogs, as long as the correct training methods are used. Dogs that like to think for themselves need consistent handling to remind them who's in charge. If you nurture a Yorkie's will to please by offering plenty of praise for good behavior,

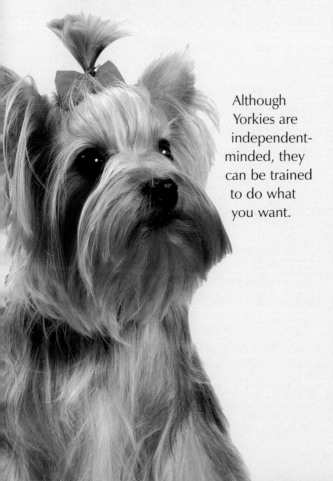

Although Yorkies are independent-minded, they can be trained to do what you want.

FAST FACT

Some Yorkies inherit an obsessively high prey drive from their terrier ancestors. These Yorkies have very little self-control when it comes to chasing things that move. They will need to be taught from the very beginning which items are not acceptable to pursue, including bicycles, vehicles, or the family cat.

that will go a long way toward creating an obedient, responsive pet.

PREY DRIVE: Combined with his independence, the Yorkie's strong prey drive gives him a true terrier psyche. Yorkshire Terriers were originally developed as ratters to hunt and kill all sorts of vermin in the mines and textile mills of nineteenth-century England. Today's Yorkie, although far removed from situations that call for the use of his skills in vermin eradication, still possesses a strong drive to pursue small animals.

Because of this, a Yorkshire Terrier may very well help keep a home free of unwanted rodents. On the flip side, however, he may not do well sharing a house with other small pets. Precautions should be taken to prevent any interspecies conflict if a Yorkie has to coexist

Despite their small size, Yorkshire Terriers enjoy taking walks and other outdoor activities.

with other animals in the same home.

A heightened prey drive can make a dog downright obsessive about chasing anything that moves, but barring such an extreme, it also provides a wonderful motivation to play. Games of chase are likely to be a Yorkie's favorite pastime, whether it's chasing balls or other toys, chasing his canine buddies, or chasing his owner.

"BIG" ATTITUDE: Strangely, the Yorkie seems oblivious to his own small size, a mental aberration perhaps bred into ratting dogs so they would not be afraid to pursue larger vermin. This trait is evident when a tiny Yorkie starts chasing a cat that's three times his size or initiates an

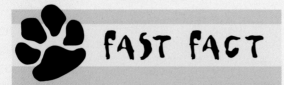

FAST FACT

Even though breed standards specify that a Yorkshire Terrier should not exceed seven pounds (3.2 kg), it's not unusual to find Yorkies that tip the scales at eight to thirteen pounds (3.6 to 5.9 kg). These dogs can make excellent choices for pets as well, especially when a larger size is preferable.

YORKIE PHYSICAL PROFILE

Weight	4–7 pounds (1.8–3.2 kg)
Height	6–9 inches (15.2–22.9 cm)
Shedding	Moderate to low
Coat Care	Daily brushing and combing
Longevity	12–15 years
Accommodations	Apartment or house with or without a yard

aggressive encounter with a dog that is large enough to swallow him whole.

At first glance, a dog that thinks he's much bigger than he really is seems cute, funny, or even entertaining, but this trait does have its drawbacks. To prevent such a dog from getting injured, it's very important to socialize him so he can learn how to behave appropriately around other dogs and animals. Because of the Yorkie's size, it is always a good idea to supervise his interactions with other animals, regardless of his familiarity with them. Even so, the Yorkie's "big" attitude adds to his innate charisma.

ENERGY LEVEL: Good behavior by a canine companion also depends on how well the dog's need for exercise

and attention is met. Dogs that don't get enough exercise and attention are unhappy dogs, and they often express their frustrations through undesirable behaviors such as destructiveness, noisemaking, or house-soiling. The good news is that it doesn't take a great deal of effort to meet a Yorkie's need for exercise.

Yorkshire Terriers have a reputation as high-energy dogs because of the way they explode with happiness when their owners come home, when it's time for a walk, or when it's time to play. But unlike other high-energy breeds, Yorkies do have an off switch. They are great for people who like an active dog, but who also like to sit back and put their feet up once in a while. Do you want a dog with the drive and tenacity to participate in a dog sport or some other favorite activity? Would you also appreciate a dog that will curl up in your lap when you want to enjoy popcorn and a movie in the evening? If so, the Yorkie may be your ideal canine companion!

JOBS YOUR YORKIE MAY ENJOY

It may sound surprising, but a Yorkie can actually make an excellent watchdog. He may think of himself as large and formidable, but the Yorkshire Terrier's diminutive stature will keep him from being promoted to the rank of protection dog. Yet very few dog breeds surpass the Yorkshire Terrier as watchdogs. According to Stanley Coren's book *The Intelligence of Dogs*, the Yorkie is the sixth-best watchdog among all the breeds recognized by the AKC.

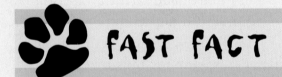 **FAST FACT**

The Yorkshire Terrier breed standards in the United States and the United Kingdom do not specify a minimum allowable size for this breed, which means the Yorkshire Terrier can be as small as genetically possible. However, adult dogs of any breed that are less than two pounds (0.9 kg) tend to suffer a great many health problems. You are best to avoid the smallest of the small when shopping for a toy dog.

Thanks to his big-dog attitude and sharp alertness, there is little that escapes the Yorkie's attention. Hopefully, you will appreciate being apprised of any happenings, for the Yorkie is an alarm system that's always on a high sensitivity setting. He'll be sure to alert you to anything happening indoors or out. In fact, his enthusiasm for his watchdog duties may have to be toned down through training.

A Yorkie should never be punished for doing a job he takes so seriously. He should be allowed to give ample warning before being told, "Quiet," and then he should be rewarded for his compliance. This way, his very effective alarm response can be better controlled.

In addition to fulfilling his watchdog duties, the Yorkie is a barker that enjoys verbal communication in general. Whether it's done to express his excitement, gain attention, or voice his displeasure, the Yorkshire Terrier is a talkative breed that should only be considered by those who appreciate (and are not so easily annoyed by) a verbally expressive dog.

Aside from watchdog duty, Yorkies also love simply being loved. The Yorkshire Terrier contains just enough spit and vinegar to make him a terrier, but he also exudes plenty of sugary sweetness, which makes him a great companion for humans. The Yorkie was purposely miniaturized so that he could live very close to people. Along the way, he was also infused with the sensitivities and empathies that make toy dogs such precious companions.

Yorkshire Terriers can be quite sensitive to their owners' emotional needs. They are exceedingly loyal and loving. So close is the bond they develop with their owners that they are often treated like children (or, in some cases, better than children). At the very least, a Yorkie manages to secure a very firm position as a valued member of the family.

Owners should be careful, however, not to allow this little terrier to take control of the household. As a terrier, the Yorkie is persistent, which means he doesn't like to take "no" for an answer. And he's independent, which means he likes to have his own way. It's only natural for a Yorkie to use his charms to get what he wants.

Partly due to this combination of personality traits and partly due to the way humans are inclined to treat small dogs, the Yorkie is at risk of becoming possessive of his favorite people, toys, or places. He can develop undesirable behaviors, such as begging or barking for attention, if his owner gives in to his demands too frequently. Even small dogs need to learn limits. Yorkies are cute, sweet, and loving, but no matter how close they become to humans, they are still dogs. Behavior that would not be tolerated in a larger dog should not be tolerated in a Yorkie, either. There is nothing wrong with treating a Yorkie like a member of the family, but he should be taught proper manners and respect. Only then will a Yorkie truly become an ideal companion.

❧❧❧

Like many other small dogs, the Yorkie is an excellent choice for apartment dwellers or those who have limited space in which to keep a dog. Even though he may appear to be fiercely independent, his strong affinity for humans means you need to lavish plenty of human attention on him. He enjoys close physical contact with his owner, but will probably prefer to experience the world from the end of a leash, rather than peeking out of a stylish tote bag. While it's important to allow him to "be a dog," safety must always be considered due to his small size.

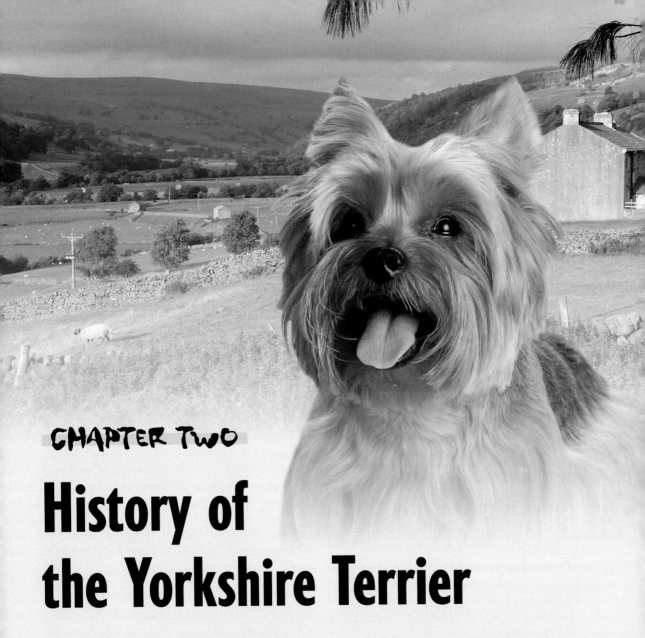

CHAPTER TWO

History of the Yorkshire Terrier

So often our attempts to improve on nature are met with dire failure, but that isn't the case with the hugely successful Yorkshire Terrier. The unique blend of traits that have made the Yorkie one of the most popular dogs in the world is the result of decades of selective breeding. The Yorkshire Terrier's building blocks may have been supplied by nature, but his construction is purely human-made.

Like many breeds, the Yorkshire Terrier developed in response to

The Yorkshire Terrier was bred in Victorian England to kill rats and other vermin.

historical events, his makeup was guided by social forces, and his temperament was molded by the desires of his human companions. Early on, the Yorkie established himself as a dual-purpose dog—part working terrier out of necessity and part companion dog out of desire. Such was the beginning of a small dog's evolution into the Yorkshire Terrier we know today.

PLACE OF ORIGIN

As its name suggests, the Yorkshire Terrier experienced considerable refinement and found its initial supporters in the northern English county of Yorkshire. But the breed's earliest ancestors are believed to have migrated there from Scotland. The end of feudalism, the decline of serfdom, and the Industrial Revolution all contributed to a gradual demographic shift. Landowners could no longer keep peasants tied to the land as serfs, which gave people greater freedom of movement. Agricultural jobs, which comprised the great majority of employment in the nineteenth century, began to decline as more efficient agricultural production methods were developed. Conversely, textile production in England flourished, due to the increased efficiency offered by the mechanization of textile mills.

FAST FACT

The word *terrier* comes from the Latin word *terra*, which means "earth" or "ground." Dogs of the type that would follow their quarry into underground burrows were referred to as "terras" or "terrarius" as early as the 15th century.

These economic factors prompted rural populations to migrate to urban areas. West Riding, one of three sections of Yorkshire County, became the second most important manufacturing area in the United Kingdom during this period. Not surprisingly, during the mid-1800s the region attracted a large influx of Scottish immigrants who were eager to take advantage of the employment opportunities.

Along with the Scots came the terriers they used for vermin control. Small dogs were less expensive to maintain, so breeding favored diminutive dogs that could do big jobs. Thus, it was common to nurture the "big" attitude of terriers through selective breeding. These small dogs could rout out and kill hundreds of rats and other vermin. In fact, they were game to take on opponents that matched or exceeded their own size.

Small but aggressive dogs that could catch and kill rats and other vermin were greatly valued in the factories of 19th-century England.

The burgeoning factories and textile mills were always in need of good ratting dogs, as sanitation was a serious and ongoing problem. Determining which dogs could perform this job most efficiently became a gruesome sport, where dogs were set upon rats in a pit similar to those used today for illegal dogfights. Dogs that proved to be excellent ratters were bred and crossbred in attempts to reproduce their desirable traits.

Some of the Scottish dogs that contributed to the development of the Yorkshire Terrier were probably Skye Terriers, which had long, straight hair and long, low builds. These dogs, however, could have erect ears or drop ears and often came in a variety of colors, so they don't much resemble the modern Yorkie's structure or color. The Paisley Terrier, a breed that was introduced to England around 1880 and is now extinct, appears to have contributed much more to the modern Yorkie's appearance. The Paisley was a small terrier with a short back and a long, silky coat that was blue on the back and tan on the legs and face.

Another extinct breed, the Clydesdale Terrier, also appears to have contributed significantly to the Yorkshire Terrier's characteristics. A little larger than the Paisley, this dog also had a silky, glossy coat. Both the Paisley and the Clydesdale were bred into other lines of dogs and eventually disappeared as distinct breeds.

FAST FACT

Before the establishment of breed clubs and registries in the late 1800s, pedigree records were sketchy and crossbreeding was a common practice. Dogs were bred for type, rather than purity of lineage. This makes it difficult to say with certainty exactly which breeds or lines of dogs contributed to the development of any breed, including the Yorkshire Terrier. We can only use common sense and deductive logic to make educated guesses and reasonable speculations.

No doubt, Scottish dogs were almost certainly crossed with English dogs over the years to create the dainty but tough terrier we know as the Yorkshire. There is some speculation that the Airedale Terrier, also originating from the West Riding in Yorkshire, may be distantly related, although the two breeds have little in common other than their coloring.

The Manchester Terrier may also have been involved in the Yorkie's development. This was a very old English terrier breed that

It's hard to believe that the primped and pampered Yorkie of today is descended from tough rat-catchers.

became quite popular in nearby Manchester in the mid-1800s. It would not be unreasonable to think that a Manchester Terrier, at one point or another, became a part of the Yorkshire Terrier's lineage.

Other breeds of dogs that have been implicated in the Yorkshire Terrier's history include the Maltese, the Dandie Dinmont Terrier, the English Black and Tan Terrier, and the Welsh Terrier. It could very well be that a great many dogs contributed genes to the Yorkie, but now it would be very difficult to tell based on physical characteristics alone.

EARLY ANCESTORS

The earliest known records of the Yorkshire Terrier are for Swift's Old Crab (sire) and Kershaw's Old Kitty (dam), which were bred in the mid-1800s. Swift's Old Crab, described as a black and tan terrier, may have been of Manchester Terrier lines, and Kershaw's Old Kitty is said to have been a Skye-type terrier.

One of the descendants of Swift's Old Crab and Kershaw's Old Kitty was Huddersfield Ben, an important dog in the development of the modern Yorkshire Terrier and often referred to as the "father" of the breed. Huddersfield Ben was considered one of the finest stud dogs in England at the time, thanks to his prepotency, or ability to pass his characteristics on to his offspring. Recognized as the foundation sire of the Yorkshire Terrier, he won many awards at dog shows and proved his superior prowess in ratting contests.

EVOLUTION OF THE BREED

It was a number of decades before the Yorkie's characteristics of size, coat type and length, and color were firmly established, partly because fanciers of the breed couldn't always agree on exactly what the Yorkshire Terrier should be. Some Yorkshire Terrier fanciers put a premium on size, while eschewing the virtues of a uniform color. Other Yorkie supporters thought hair was the dog's primary defining characteristic.

Just about the only thing Yorkshire Terrier enthusiasts have always agreed on is the deportment that should be shown by this lovely little dog. The Yorkie's spunky attitude and sporty approach to life were always cited as requirements for keeping terrier as part of the Yorkie's identity.

Ben was born in 1865 and met a premature death in 1871, when he was run over by a carriage. Despite his short life, his impact on the Yorkshire Terrier breed was tremendous. He was so greatly respected that his body was preserved and placed on display to be admired long after his death.

Although dog shows were growing popular during this period, registries and breed clubs had not yet been established to provide governance over the shows or guidelines for the individual breeds. Dogs were classified by type, and the Yorkshire Terrier was referred to as a "Broken-haired Scotch or Yorkshire Terrier."

The simplified name of Yorkshire Terrier became generally accepted after one of Ben's sons, Mozart, won first place in a Variety Class at a Westmoreland dog show around 1870. A reporter covering the show for *The Field* wrote, "They ought no longer to be called Scotch Terriers but Yorkshire Terriers." The name has been used ever since.

DEVELOPMENT OF THE YORKSHIRE TERRIER

Even though Huddersfield Ben was a prominent sire of smaller Yorkies, the size of many Yorkies still fluctuated between three and thirteen pounds (1.4 and 5.9 kg) in the show

The Yorkie breed gradually evolved from tough working dog to pampered house pet.

ring. The Yorkshire Terrier's tiny stature of seven pounds (3.2 kg) or less was not a consistent characteristic until the 1930s. This may have been due to the practice of classifying dogs according to size at dog shows. Toy dogs (those five pounds [2.2 kg] or less) were classified separately.

Yorkshire Terriers could be shown under the classifications of "Not Exceeding 5 Pounds" or "Over 5 Pounds" for many years. We can safely assume that Yorkies came in different sizes simply because they were allowed to be different sizes. These different size classifications applied even after the Yorkshire Terrier was recognized as a distinct breed by the American Kennel Club (AKC) and the Kennel Club (KC) in the late 1800s.

The Yorkshire Terrier's distinctive coat also went through a transformation as the breed's evolution progressed. Descending from Scottish ancestors with long, straight hair of a coarser texture, the Yorkshire Terrier's coat acquired a more silky-fine texture over time. Huddersfield Ben is credited with having improved the

Yorkshire's coat quality, while successive generations produced even greater length. So much attention is now focused on the Yorkie's coat qualities that a third of the AKC breed standard is devoted to it!

THE YORKSHIRE TERRIER IN ENGLAND

The Kennel Club (KC) first recognized the Yorkshire Terrier as a distinct breed in 1886, and the Yorkshire Terrier Club in England was formed in 1898. One of the most influential people in the development of the breed during its early years was Lady Edith Wyndham-Dawson, who served as secretary of the Yorkshire Terrier Club and spent decades breeding Yorkies to obtain the most desirable characteristics.

There were only 300 Yorkshire Terriers registered with the KC by 1932. But it was only a matter of time before the Yorkie's charm captured the public's attention. By the 1970s, the Yorkie had become the most popular breed in all of Britain. The modern Yorkie continues to maintain a respectable rank in popularity throughout the United Kingdom.

THE YORKSHIRE TERRIER IN THE UNITED STATES

The first Yorkshire Terriers were imported to the United States in

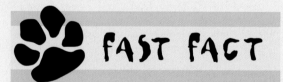

FAST FACT

During the Yorkshire Terrier's long period of development, the breed was known by a number of different names, including Halifax Terrier, Blue Fawn Terrier, and Broken-haired Scotch or Yorkshire Terrier.

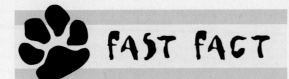

FAST FACT

The modern Yorkie's excessively long coat has obviously been exaggerated through decades of selective breeding, but the Yorkie's predecessors, like many terriers of the past, had medium-length coats—long enough so that the dogs could be grasped by their hair to pull them out of their quarries' holes.

1872 and were subsequently recognized by the AKC in 1878. The first Yorkie to achieve an American championship was Bradford Harry in 1889. Not surprisingly, he was the great-great-grandson of Huddersfield Ben. But despite this early success, it took the breed some time to become established in the United States.

Beginning in the 1960s and continuing through the 1970s, the Yorkshire Terrier experienced a population boom, as evidenced by its registration statistics with the AKC. With an average of less than 200 registrations per year before the end of World War II, the Yorkie blossomed to 13,000 registrations in 1970. The Yorkie has continued to draw a lot of interest in the United States ever since, becoming the second most registered breed of dog in 2006. The current popularity of toy dogs in general is sure to keep the Yorkie in favor with Americans for some time to come.

MASCOT AND HERO

The heart and spirit of the Yorkie can best be revealed through the story of Smokey, a Yorkshire Terrier who became the mascot and hero of American soldiers during World War II. The four-pound (1.8 kg) purebred Yorkie was found shivering in a shell hole during fighting between the Americans and the Japanese in the New Guinea jungle. She was adopted by William Wynne, a U.S. Army aerial photographer from Cleveland, who unsuccessfully tried to establish her origins. Japanese prisoners of war did not recognize her, and she didn't seem to respond to spoken Japanese or English.

Small enough to travel in a soldier's pack, she accompanied Wynne on 150 air raids and twelve air-sea rescue missions. Her tiny size and terrier instincts proved quite valuable when the Signal Corps had to lay a telegraph wire through an eight-inch (20 cm) pipe under an airstrip at Lingayen. Smokey crawled through the 70-foot (21 meter) pipe with a tow line that was used to pull the telegraph wire through the pipe.

Smokey and Wynne traveled to many Army and Navy hospitals

around the world to entertain and cheer up soldiers, even after the war was over. This little dog was the perfect example of how the Yorkshire Terrier's size, spirit, and companionship qualities have created a very special breed of dog.

BREED STANDARDS AND CONFORMATION

The establishment of a breed club is critical to a breed's survival, a fact that was recognized by early Yorkshire Terrier fanciers. A breed club is responsible for drawing up the breed standard that encourages the consistency of characteristics for the breed. It unites breed fanciers with common goals, promotes the breed to the public, and addresses serious issues that affect the breed. Before the establishment of breed clubs in the late 1800s, the physical characteristics of most breeds of dog were loosely defined, but thanks to the Yorkshire Terrier clubs in America and abroad, the Yorkshire Terrier has become a unique and recognizable dog breed.

The Yorkshire Terrier breed standard contains lengthy descriptions of size, color, body structure, and conformation of the head, legs, and tail. These guidelines provide a template of the ideal Yorkshire Terrier, so that breeders can attempt to meet this ideal by breeding dogs with the correct characteristics.

The breed standard does more than describe a beautiful dog. The conformation outlined in a breed standard often evolves just as much out of practical considerations as it does aesthetics. Conformation affects a dog's balance, coordination, movement, and general health. Dogs that are constructed properly are less likely to suffer lameness, back problems, or arthritis. So even if you are not interested in showing your Yorkshire Terrier, it is still wise to purchase a dog with good breeding.

SIZE: According to the American Kennel Club (AKC) and the Kennel Club of the United Kingdom (KC) breed standards, the weight of the Yorkshire Terrier should not exceed seven pounds (3.2 kg). This makes the Yorkie small, even for a toy dog. Yorkshire Terriers make excellent pets for those who want to enjoy the many benefits of having a miniaturized canine. Small dogs don't take up much room on the bed or couch, they don't eat much, and they don't produce much waste. Their modest demands for space make them particularly well suited for apartment living or traveling. Even when in full coat, they shed less hair than larger dogs as well.

Although the Yorkshire Terrier's tiny stature has many benefits, it can also present some problems. Because the Yorkie can be easily carried, he can also be dropped, which puts this small dog at risk of injury. Care should be taken when handling Yorkies, and children, in particular, should be supervised when interacting with them. Most toy dogs, including the Yorkie, are not recommended for families with children under the age of ten. Most children under ten lack the knowledge, skills, and coordination to handle such a small dog properly, and they're not always aware that their actions can cause pain and injury to a dog.

COAT: Beautiful to behold and pleasant to touch, the Yorkie's long hair adds a flair of elegance to this scrappy little terrier. You might consider the Yorkie a hybrid between a prince and a pauper, with enough qualities of each to please those of either class. But the lovely hair that represents one of his more royal qualities tends to require just as much royal attention.

Beauty always comes with a price, and in this case, that means daily brushing and cleaning. Woe to the long-haired Yorkie that does not receive doting attention to his coat, as his floor-length fur will tangle into uncomfortable mats. Food will also remain encrusted around his mouth and, worst of all, waste may adhere to the tresses under his tail!

Fortunately, the Yorkie can easily be adapted to a more practical lifestyle by having his hair trimmed by a professional groomer. A haircut will leave the Yorkie more fluffy than silky, giving him an appealing, puppylike appearance. Trading

Purebred Yorkshire Terriers are judged on the quality of their coats. It's impossible to keep a Yorkie looking this good without daily brushing, however!

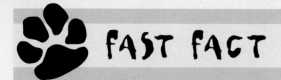

FAST FACT

The coat of Yorkshire Terriers changes from a black-and-tan color pattern when they're puppies to a blue-and-tan color pattern when they reach adulthood. According to the Yorkshire Terrier Club of America, this color change can occur over the course of three years or more.

elegance for cuteness isn't such a bad deal, especially if it contributes to the health and comfort of the dog.

As a testament to his versatility, a Yorkie can be kept as either a long-haired or medium-haired dog. In either case, however, you have to invest time into the care of the Yorkie's coat. He can have his cloak of hair meticulously tended or regularly trimmed.

The traditional long-haired Yorkie has his straight hair parted down the middle of his back to fall down each side of his body. In the interest of hygiene and neatness, the body hair is often trimmed at the bottom to prevent it from dragging too much on the floor, and the hair on the feet is trimmed to a tidy length. The hair on the Yorkie's head and face is allowed to grow long, with the fall (the hair on the top of the head) either pulled up into a bow at the peak of the crown or parted down the middle and secured by two bows, one on each side of the crown. Without a bow or another form of tie, the hair on the top of the head is traditionally parted down the middle to fall to either side of the head, away from the eyes. The treatment of the fall is more than just a fashion statement, as the Yorkie's long hair can easily fall over his eyes and impair his vision.

Shortly cropped Yorkies are usually trimmed an even length all over, with the legs, feet, and body hair cut to about one-half to one inch (13mm–2.5cm) in length. The face is trimmed into a youthfully round shape. Although this would never be acceptable in the show ring, it's quite practical for house pets and may even be preferable for those who like a less opulent look.

COLOR: This is one characteristic that doesn't allow much variation, as the Yorkshire Terrier breed standard is very specific with regard to acceptable coloring and shading.

Yorkshire Terrier puppies are born black and tan, with black hairs infiltrating much of the tan areas. The invasive black hairs recede with maturity, until the tan areas become completely pure. The black areas soften into a steel blue color as the

Color is an important element of the Yorkie breed standard. Over time, this Yorkie pup's coat will lose its black hairs and become the proper tan shade.

pup grows older. According to the breed standard, the adult Yorkie displays this blue color from the back of his neck to the base of his tail, with the tail hair growing in a slightly darker shade of blue than that on the body. Tan hair on the head, chest, and legs is darkest at the roots and lightest at the tips, with darker shades also noted at the sides of the head, the base of the ears, and on the muzzle. The tan on the legs must not advance beyond the elbows of the front legs or the stifles of the rear legs.

Such strict, descriptive color requirements illustrate the importance of color in the Yorkshire Terrier breed. It is not unreasonable to judge the quality of a Yorkie's breeding by noting how closely he meets these color requirements.

GENERAL APPEARANCE AND STRUCTURE: Regardless of the physical image his hairdo imparts, the Yorkshire Terrier's carriage and structure reveal a confident little dog with a terrier's vigor and a distinct sense of self-importance. His head is carried high, a sign of alertness and courage, and his tail, which is cropped to a medium length, is held slightly higher than the level of his back, proof of his terrier boldness.

The Yorkshire Terrier's body is very well proportioned, which contributes to his coordination and balance. You won't find any exaggerated features on the Yorkie's frame, and this makes him quite a nimble canine specimen. He definitely has no problem jumping onto furniture three times his own height to fulfill his duties as a lapdog!

CHAPTER THREE

Responsible Pet Ownership

Once you enter the world of pet ownership, you'll notice that people treat you differently. Perfect strangers will begin to greet you and talk to you when you're out walking your Yorkie. Other dog lovers will start sharing their doggy passions with you a little more openly when they find out you have a Yorkie. But before you start basking too comfortably in all this new attention, be aware that reactions to your

Dog owners must keep their pets under control at all times when they are out in public.

new dog will not be so positive if you don't observe the etiquette of responsible pet ownership.

Obviously, as a pet owner you're charged with the responsibilities of caring for your dog properly, training him, and keeping him safe. But you're also expected to abide by the laws of your community and make sure that your Yorkie conducts himself in socially accepted ways. If you do, even those people who have no affinity for dogs will happily accept your dog as a member of the community.

IDENTIFICATION

One of the most important things you can do as a responsible dog owner is to provide your Yorkie with a form of identification so that he can be returned to you if he's ever lost or stolen. If you think your little Yorkie is too dependent on you to ever wander off, you've forgotten about his tenacious terrier instinct to pursue squirrels or other small animals. Many a small terrier has found his way to the stray ward of an animal shelter or animal control agency.

No dog should be without a collar and ID tag. If your dog is intended for show, you might cringe at the thought of the tangles and broken hairs a collar might cause in your Yorkie's pristine coat, but a collar doesn't have to be worn every day. A smooth, cordlike nylon collar is less likely to cause hair damage, and you can use it only when you take your dog for walks, while traveling, or on other outings.

For additional protection, your dog should have some form of permanent ID. Unlike collars and ID tags, microchips and tattoos cannot be removed or fall off. A microchip is a tiny computer chip your veterinarian can inject under the skin between your dog's shoulder blades. This chip can then be detected by a scanner held over your dog's back. Microchips have become so common that most veterinary clinics and animal shelters automatically check stray dogs for microchips.

It's a good idea to get a collar with sturdy fasteners to ensure that it doesn't fall off your dog.

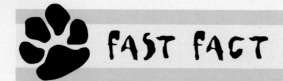

Pet theft is a real issue. Animal welfare agencies estimate that 1.5 to 2 million dogs and cats are stolen in the United States every year.

Tattoos have become less popular since the advent of microchips, but some people still prefer them. The one advantage they have over microchips is that no scanner is required to detect them. A veterinarian in your area may be qualified to apply tattoos, which are virtually painless to dogs (their skin structure is different than ours). A tattoo can be put on the inside of your dog's rear leg, on his stomach, or on the underside of his ear. The tattoo is then registered with a tattoo registry, which will notify you if your lost dog is found.

LICENSING

A license tag can be used to reunite you with your stray dog, but that isn't their only purpose. Licensing helps your local government control and manage the dog population in your community. It helps your community enforce pet-related ordinances, such as those that pertain to dogs at large or the number of dogs allowed per household. Most important, licensing makes it possible to keep track of which dogs have been vaccinated for rabies. Such controls not only make your community a safer place for people to live, they also make it a better place for dogs.

CANINE POPULATION CONTROL

One of the most pressing issues facing animal welfare today is the overpopulation of dogs and cats. The population of pets has so outgrown the number of available homes that 5 million dogs and cats are needlessly destroyed each year, according to estimates by the Humane Society of the United States. The problem has become so overwhelming that legislation is currently being considered in several states that would severely limit or control pet owners' rights to breed their animals, including those animals intended for show. Such legislation would not be necessary if

Pet overpopulation isn't just an animal welfare issue. According to People for the Ethical Treatment of Animals, it costs taxpayers an estimated $2 billion a year to capture, house, kill, and dispose of homeless animals.

DISPELLING MYTHS

The best thing you can do as an individual to help combat the problem of pet overpopulation is to help dispel the following myths about spaying and neutering of pets:

Myth: Neutering or spaying will affect my dog's personality.

Truth: Your Yorkie will have the same sweet, loving personality after neutering or spaying. Sterilization surgery has no effect on personality, but it does help eliminate annoying sexual behaviors, such as roaming and marking territory (urinating) in the house.

Myth: Neutering or spaying will cause my dog to gain weight.

Truth: Weight gain in a healthy dog is strictly related to diet and exercise. Some dogs may become slightly less active after sterilization surgery, as they will not be expending as much energy on sexual matters, but a proper diet and adequate exercise will compensate for this.

Myth: It's better for my dog to have one litter before spaying.

Truth: Having a litter prior to spaying has no health or behavioral benefits for your dog. On the contrary, there are serious health risks involved in pregnancy and birth, especially when things don't go exactly as nature intended.

Myth: Neutering my male dog will strip him of his masculinity.

Truth: Neutered male dogs still have typical male characteristics—larger size, broader head, and bolder personalities than females—but these differences are not as pronounced in the Yorkshire Terrier breed as in other breeds to begin with. The only "maleness" eliminated by neutering your Yorkie is his desire to search for mates.

more pet owners did their part to prevent pet overpopulation.

There are very few legitimate reasons to breed a dog. If you're interested in showing your dog or passing on your dog's fine traits, breeding may be a serious consideration. But keep in mind that conscientious breeders care about each and every puppy they produce. They take whatever steps are necessary to ensure that all the puppies are placed in good homes, and they are willing to take back and re-home any of the puppies at any time during their lives, if necessary. Are you willing to make

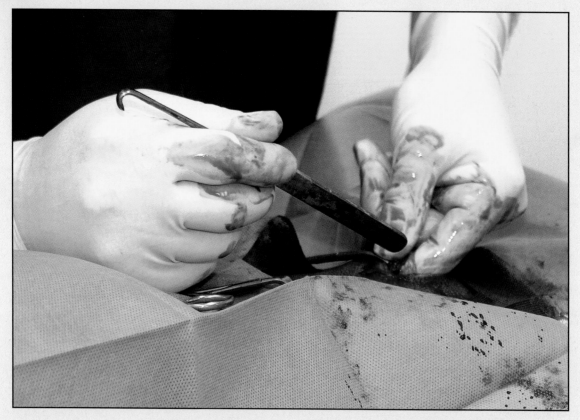

Choosing whether or not to spay or neuter your dog is an important decision. According to the Humane Society of the United States, one female dog and her offspring can theoretically produce up to 67,000 dogs in six years!

such a strong commitment to the puppies you bring into the world?

In most cases, unfortunately, dogs are bred for all the wrong reasons. Some people think having a litter of puppies will be fun, only to find out that it's a messy, labor-intensive experience. Some think they can make money by breeding their Yorkshire Terrier, since Yorkies are very popular small dogs. But then they discover the exorbitant costs of veterinary care when their pregnant

bitch requires a C-section, or they are totally unprepared for the expense of vaccinating a whole litter of puppies. Some people just want to experience, or have their children experience, the miracle of life. But the puppies resulting from such "experiments" are the ones most likely to be considered "throwaways" and end up in animal shelters and rescue organizations.

Strangely, the one disadvantage many people do not think about

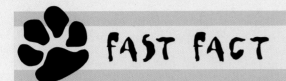

FAST FACT

Research by the National Council on Pet Population Study and Policy indicates that intact dogs are more likely to be relinquished to animal shelters. Dogs that participate in obedience training are less likely to be relinquished.

when they consider breeding their dogs is that intact dogs do not always make the best pets. Intact male dogs may be more aggressive than neutered males, thanks to a higher level of testosterone. They are more likely to roam in search of a mate and to urinate in the house to mark their territory. Intact female dogs aren't much better. Their bi-annual heat cycles are characterized by a messy, bloody discharge and flirty, skittish, or anxious behavior. So unless your Yorkie has something special to add to the Yorkie gene pool, you, your neighbors, and the world of dogs will all be better off if you neuter or spay your pet.

LEGAL ISSUES

Many of your duties as a responsible dog owner revolve around acceptable social etiquette. Adhering to such unspoken and unwritten rules helps us all respect each other and live in

harmony. In other words, they civilize us. But there are occasions when a pet owner's responsibility is far too important to leave its execution to goodwill. In this case, a law is enacted to ensure compliance. Leash laws, nuisance laws, and general liability laws exist to create a safe environment for humans and dogs alike.

LEASH LAWS: Many communities have leash laws that require you to keep your dog on a leash any time you leave your home. These laws are designed to encourage dog owners to keep their dogs under

Your Yorkie will probably have to be kept on a leash when he's in public areas.

control at all times. If a dog is found running at large, a leash law gives law enforcement agencies the right to impose fines on the owner for noncompliance.

It's easy to see why such laws are necessary if you envision large dogs running loose and terrorizing the neighborhood children, but this law applies to your little Yorkie, too! Despite his seemingly harmless size, a Yorkie at large can still run into a street and cause a serious motor vehicle accident. He can cause property damage by digging up the neighbor's tulips, even if he was only trying to capture the mole he heard

scurrying around underground. And, small as he is, he's capable of inflicting a pretty nasty bite, even if he's justifiably scared and defensive. Such scenarios can be avoided by keeping your dog confined or leashed, and under your control at all times.

NUISANCE LAWS: Your community may also have an ordinance that applies to nuisance issues. Restrictions on the level or frequency of noise and the visual impact of eyesores are necessary so that people can live in close proximity to each other without conflict. The most common type of nuisance dogs

You may have to train your Yorkie to control his barking, particularly if you live in an apartment, a townhouse, or another place where it might annoy your neighbors.

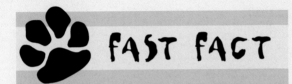

FAST FACT

In 2007 the AKC began encouraging its member clubs to support a Responsible Dog Ownership Day during the month of September to draw attention to the importance of responsible dog ownership.

create is noise. All dogs bark, but some dogs bark louder and longer than others.

Yorkshire Terriers are notorious barkers. Some Yorkies let out a fervent series of yelps every time someone walks by the house, or even when they hear the sump pump kick in. This behavior was bred into the Yorkie as part of his vermin-hunting responsibilities. Terriers that chased their quarry into the ground were strong barkers; this made it easy for their owners to determine where they were located. The dogs or their prey could then be dug up, if necessary. This trait was useful if the dog had gotten himself into a tough spot or if the dog needed help in dispatching his game.

The good news is that the Yorkie is a small dog with a moderate bark. The barking he does within the confines of your home is unlikely to disturb your neighbors, unless you live in an apartment. It's still in your best interest to teach your Yorkie to control his barking. To be fair to your dog, you must allow him to bark a sufficient warning before asking him to "quiet." Each time he quiets down at your request, reward him with plenty of praise, and he will soon learn to limit his noisemaking.

LIABILITY: Learning how to control your dog's behavior is a very important part of dog ownership. There are some people who think training their dogs is optional, but the law doesn't see things that way. You are legally responsible for everything you own, including your dog. If your dog bites someone or causes any type of property damage, the liability is yours.

The highly litigious state of modern society makes it a priority to teach your dog how to behave appropriately. You should want to learn everything you can about how to control and manage your dog's behavior. Chapter seven of this book includes instructions on how to train your Yorkie to follow basic commands. Beyond this, you should consult other books for advanced training or enroll your dog in obedience training classes. Most importantly, consult a professional when you need help to solve a problem.

CHAPTER FOUR

The Best Possible Beginning

In order to grow the best garden, a gardener must first choose good seeds. He must plant them where the soil is rich, or else all his care and tending will be in vain. Likewise, a good start for you and your Yorkshire Terrier depends on the choices and preparations that you and your family make before your Yorkie even joins the household.

CHOOSING THE RIGHT YORKIE FOR YOU

Yorkshire Terriers may all look pretty much the same, but they aren't. There are different genders, many

Before you become a dog owner, you and your family will have to make some important decisions about the kind of Yorkshire Terrier that you want.

different ages, slightly different personalities, and enormously different price tags, as the quality of their breeding can range from accidental to championship bloodlines. Your needs, wants, and expectations should help you determine which Yorkie is the best for you. Considering even the small details can make all the difference between a good match and a great match between you and your dog!

GENDER: The most basic element to consider is whether you want a male or female dog. Both male and female Yorkies inherit the characteristically sweet, loving, and spirited temperament that has been bred into them for over a century. Because of this, most Yorkies, regardless of their gender, can make wonderful, devoted pets. So what difference does sex make?

In the case of neutered or spayed Yorkies kept strictly as pets, gender is really nothing more than a personal preference. But choosing between a male and a female becomes a much more serious decision if you plan to keep your Yorkie intact for showing or breeding purposes. Intact dogs of both genders engage in hormone-driven behaviors that can make them a challenge to live with. They may develop the habit of wandering in search of a mate or scent marking (urinating) in the home. Male dogs, who are always ready for sexual encounters, constantly engage in these behaviors; females, who come into heat twice per year, have seasonal sexually driven behavior.

If you choose to take on the responsibilities of owning a breeding dog, you need to consider the drawbacks of each sex. If you choose a stud dog, are you willing to take someone else's female dogs into your home for breeding? If you choose a female, are you prepared to entrust

Yorkies make great pets whether they are male or female.

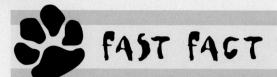

FAST FACT

It may not seem fair, but when it comes to sterilization surgery there is no equality between the sexes. It costs more to spay a female dog than to neuter a male dog because spay surgery is much more invasive and risky. This also means that females may require a slightly longer recovery period.

your dog to a stud dog owner for breeding? Are you willing to care and pay for a pregnant female and spend up to ten weeks raising a litter of puppies? One pup can be a challenge for a new dog owner; an entire litter may be overwhelming.

PUPPY OR ADULT DOG: The age of your Yorkie will have a huge impact on the effort required from you as an owner. Yorkshire Terrier puppies are itsy bitsy balls of cuteness. They are fun and playful, and they have more charm in their stubby little tails than most dogs have in their whole bodies. However, although it's a very rewarding experience to raise a Yorkshire Terrier from puppyhood, it does require a considerable commitment of time.

Puppies need to be trained and socialized. They need constant supervision, and they need to be fed

more frequently, let outside more frequently, and cleaned up after more frequently than adult dogs. Most Yorkie lovers consider the time spent raising a Yorkie to be just as much fun as it is work, but you need to have that time to begin with.

Puppies also require a greater monetary investment in health care than adult dogs. The costs of vaccinations, wormings, and sterilization surgery can be significant. Before acquiring a puppy, it's a good idea to shop around among nearby

Raising a puppy involves a lot of work, but for many people the cuddles make all of the effort worthwhile.

FAST FACT

It can be very rewarding to watch a tiny Yorkshire Terrier pup grow up from a palm-sized ball of fluff to an elegant and self-assured adult. But the operative word here is tiny. Yorkies are exceptionally small as adults, but they are minuscule as puppies. Can you keep such a teeny creature safe from harm? You must be very diligent, and maybe even a little overprotective, if you want to be a pet parent to a Yorkie pup! For families with young children, an adult Yorkie may be a better choice.

veterinarians to figure out how much all these procedures will cost, and make sure they are within your means. Then, if a puppy still seems like a good idea, go ahead and let yourself fall crazy in love with the idea of puppy-rearing!

As easy as it is to become enchanted by a spunky, baby bunny–sized Yorkie puppy, it's also hard to ignore the benefits of getting an adult Yorkie. Adult Yorkies can be found through shelters, rescue organizations, or breeders. Most of them have already been vaccinated and neutered or spayed. They should already be housetrained. Best of all, they will have outgrown the highly destructive teething stage!

There's always the possibility that an adult dog has developed some undesirable behaviors outside your control, but most behavior issues can be solved with consistent training and proper management. When you consider the amount of training that goes into raising a puppy, retraining an adult dog is certainly no more challenging. The important thing is to keep a list of helpful resources handy. Dog trainers, veterinarians, animal behavior consultants, animal shelters, and rescue organizations are all great sources of information and advice. They can help you through any difficult training or developmental issue with your Yorkie, regardless of your dog's age.

EVALUATING A PUPPY OR AN ADULT DOG

No matter the gender or age, each dog is an individual. One pup might have the potential to wow judges in the show ring, while another has the makings of a superior pet. One Yorkie might have the energy and drive to excel in Agility competitions, while another prefers the more placid task of therapy work. Each dog has his own strengths and weaknesses, so you need to consider which traits are most important to you.

Some of the most prominent canine personality traits you should

DETERMINING YOUR PUPPY'S APTITUDE

The potential for a puppy to fill any specific role has been turned into something of a science. Jack and Wendy Volhard, well-respected dog trainers and authors, have devised the Puppy Aptitude Test to make it easier to evaluate puppies. The test, in its entirety, can be viewed on their Web site, www.volhard.com. Psychologist and canine intelligence expert Stanley Coren developed both a Canine IQ Test and an Obedience Personality Test, which are outlined in his book *The Intelligence of Dogs*. If you have specific goals for your poodle puppy, consider evaluating him using one or more of these methods.

consider are submissiveness/dominance, prey drive, and energy level. These canine personality traits have a very strong influence on how well a particular Yorkshire Terrier will meet your goals. They affect a Yorkie's potential as a pet, a sport dog, even a show dog. And because these traits are inherited, they are fixed characteristics. A submissive dog will always be a submissive dog, a dog with a high prey drive will always have a high prey drive, and a dog with a high energy level will always have a high energy level.

All dogs fall somewhere on the submissiveness/dominance scale, but for most purposes, you should avoid extremes. Overly submissive dogs may be too timid to fulfill most expectations, and they are at a higher risk for developing fear aggression, a form of hostile or belligerent behavior rooted in fear. Overly dominant dogs are difficult to control and are at a higher risk for becoming dominant aggressive; that is, exhibiting aggressiveness that stems from a genetic predisposition for dominance.

FAST FACT

Personality is the strongest predictor of future behavior. Avoid dogs that display personality extremes, such as fearfulness, nervousness, or aggressiveness. Most experts recommend choosing a dog that falls somewhere in the middle on the personality scale—friendly but not too bold, submissive but not fearful, and playful but not insanely wild.

The Yorkshire Terrier is always endowed with a fairly high amount of prey drive, thanks to his history as a rat hunter. But individuals do vary in the level of prey drive they possess, and this can be a very important consideration, depending on your situation. If you want a dog that will participate enthusiastically in the sport of Flyball, you'll want a Yorkie with a higher prey drive. If you want a dog that will get along with your cat, you may want to search for Yorkies that fall lower on the prey drive scale.

Yorkies are also known to have a good supply of energy: it is rare to find a lazy terrier. But some Yorkies are absolutely bursting with effervescence, while others fall into the moderate energy range. Highly excitable Yorkies might do well on the sport dog circuit, but the job of therapy dog work should be reserved for the calmer Yorkies, who are better able to control their exuberance when they meet new people.

So once you have decided on the level of submissiveness/dominance, prey drive, and energy level that are appropriate for your needs, how can you tell if a puppy or adult dog has the right stuff for you? One way is to use your own powers of observation to determine which puppies in

a litter appear to be bolder or shyer, more energetic or calmer, or possess more tenacity or less concern in pursuing things that move. But the easiest way is to ask the breeder, who has been observing the puppies since they were born and can provide insights into the personality of each individual pup.

EVALUATING PHYSICAL TRAITS

Evaluating physical traits is particularly crucial in choosing a potential show dog. If you yearn for the challenges and rewards of canine Conformation competition, you need to study the Yorkshire Terrier breed standard with a passion. It

FAST FACT

Because physical traits change dramatically as puppies grow, it is almost impossible to determine whether or not an eight-week-old puppy will fare well in the show ring. Breeders who are serious about raising show prospects will often keep their puppies until they are three or four months old. At this age, it's easier to see which puppies have inherited the physical traits necessary to do well in Conformation competition. Don't expect to obtain a very young puppy if showing is your goal.

takes some time and practice to develop an eye for correct conformation, so until you reach expert status, you're wise to seek the advice of those who are more experienced.

You can find breeders or mentors who are willing to help you get started in the sport of showing purebred dogs by contacting your local Yorkshire Terrier breed club. Obtaining assistance in choosing your first show dog prospect can be invaluable and will contribute greatly to your success in the show ring.

Evaluating for physical traits may seem like a useless endeavor if you don't intend to show your Yorkie in competition, but that's not entirely true. Yorkshire Terriers with slight flaws in coloring, size, or structure can still make excellent pets, but

Not all Yorkies are created equal. Even dogs from the same litter will have different appearances and personalities.

radical flaws can lead to serious health concerns. Avoid purchasing a Yorkie that's obviously the result of poor breeding. Excessively long backs, crooked legs, poor coat quality, or other physical defects can cause future problems. If a Yorkie exhibits such obvious outer signs of poor breeding, you have to wonder what internal defects may exist as well, and these are much harder to detect.

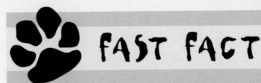

FAST FACT

Want a good reason why you should have your puppy tested and treated for worms? Almost all dogs are infected with roundworms at birth, and these parasites are easily transmitted to humans, according to the National Institutes of Health, U.S. Dept. of Health and Human Services.

EVALUATING A YORKIE'S HEALTH

It's impossible to detect latent hereditary defects simply by looking at a dog or puppy. That's why it's important to find out if the puppies in a litter or their parents have been tested for any inheritable diseases. There are not yet tests for every genetic problem that affects dogs, but it doesn't hurt to rule out as many potential problems as possible. For Yorkshire Terriers, this may include Canine Eye Research Foundation (CERF) screening for any eye problems, x-rays to detect the presence of Legg-Calve-Perthes disease, a patellar luxation test recommended by the Orthopedic Foundation for Animals (OFA), and a blood test to detect a bleeding disorder called von Willebrand's disease.

Evaluating a puppy's general health is just as important. If any

single puppy in a litter shows signs of illness, such as squinty or teary eyes, discharge from the nose, or lethargy, all the puppies in the litter have been exposed to the underlying illness. Other signs to watch for include a dull, thin coat or flaky skin. Bald patches may indicate a mange infestation, excessive scratching may be a sign of fleas, and a bloated belly is an indication of intestinal worms.

When it comes to health, the very best beginning for your puppy starts long before you bring him home. Puppies that appear to be clean, healthy, and robust have obviously received the best of care from their breeder. Even mild symptoms of illness are something to worry about. (See chapter six, "Your Yorkie's Health," for further information on health issues affecting Yorkshire Terriers.)

WHERE TO FIND A YORKSHIRE TERRIER

It's always desirable to obtain a Yorkshire Terrier from a quality source. But while superior bloodlines may be a priority in some cases, it's not always necessary or affordable in other cases. Again, your particular situation will determine the best place to look for the Yorkshire Terrier of your dreams.

If you want a Yorkshire Terrier that can reach the pinnacle of dogdom by achieving the coveted title of Conformation Champion, you'll need to buy a puppy from the best source you can find, from the best stock you can afford. But if you want a pet-quality Yorkie at a more affordable price, you can consider purchasing a dog from a reputable hobby breeder.

Any reputable breeder will take great care to give her puppies the best possible start in life. Puppies need a clean environment in which to thrive. They should have plenty of room to move around and plenty of toys and attention to stimulate them mentally and physically. Socialization to people, other animals, and children is highly desirable.

A breeder who takes his or her duties seriously keeps excellent records. Registration papers should be in order, and vaccination records

PAPERS YOUR BREEDER SHOULD SUPPLY

American Kennel Club registration papers—These are necessary to register the dog or puppy in your name.

Pedigree—This is a chart of the dog's or puppy's family tree. The availability of this information shows that the breeder is serious about keeping meticulous records of her breeding program.

Puppy sale contract—Reputable breeders issue puppy sale contracts to help ensure the welfare of the puppies they sell. The advantages for puppy buyers is that these contracts help avoid misunderstandings by outlining the responsibilities of both the breeder and the buyer, and they note, in writing, any health guarantees.

Health records—These should document any veterinary care your dog or puppy has received, including vaccinations, wormings, medications and surgeries.

A reputable breeder will begin the process of socializing her Yorkies several weeks before you'll be able to take a puppy home.

for the puppies should be up-to-date. Do not take a breeder's word that registration papers will be "forthcoming." In most cases, this means the breeder has neglected to register the puppies. Reputable breeders often require a contract of sale that spells out the kind of care they expect the puppy to receive and what kind of health guarantees the buyer can expect.

Any breeder who cannot produce at least one of the puppies' parents for inspection should be suspect. In some cases, this means the breeder is really a broker who purchases puppies from questionable sources to resell. The puppies in such a situation may also be the products of puppy mills, which are dog breeding operations that engage in questionable breeding practices. Puppy mills not only produce inferior-quality puppies that have been known to suffer from a wide range of health and behavioral problems, they are also criticized for keeping their breeding dogs and puppies in deplorable conditions. If you can't verify where a puppy originated, it's best to find a puppy from another source.

ADOPTING FROM A SHELTER OR RESCUE ORGANIZATION

A great place to look for companion dogs is your local shelter. You will not find a Best of Breed contender among the ranks of shelter dogs, and Yorkies from such a humble background may very well be the products of unscrupulous breeders, but there is no bond of gratitude stronger than that offered by a "secondhand" dog. Many Yorkie lovers have experienced the myriad rewards of giving a homeless Yorkie a second chance in life.

Shelter dogs may not have registration papers, well-documented health histories, or superb breeding, but they do offer many other advantages. The greatest advantage of getting a Yorkie from a shelter is affordability. Most shelters include the costs of vaccinations and neutering or spaying in their adoption fees. Some even include heartworm testing and microchips.

Shelter dogs are often screened for health and temperament, so any issues in these areas are placed upfront and won't appear as surprises once you bring your dog home. The requirements and adoption contracts of some shelters may seem stringent, but shelters are only concerned with providing the best homes for their dogs. They don't want to see the animal come back and have to languish there while waiting for another owner to come along.

Perhaps the only real disadvantage of adopting a Yorkie from a shelter is availability. Even though a quarter of the dogs taken in by shelters are purebreds, it may be difficult to find a Yorkshire Terrier. Small dogs are in high demand and tend to be adopted quickly. Your best bet is to ask to be added to a waiting list so the shelter can contact you when the right dog becomes available.

If shelters don't have the breed you're looking for, consider contacting a rescue organization. Besides offering many of the same benefits as shelters, Yorkie rescue groups are a great source of information and advice because of their experience with the breed. Another advantage is that rescue dogs are most often kept in foster homes rather than kennels. This means the dogs can be observed in a home environment, and more reliable assessments can be made regarding their personalities and behavior. All these elements contribute to a greater chance of successfully placing rescued dogs in new homes.

Yorkshire Terrier rescue groups can be found by contacting the Yorkshire Terrier Club of America or by checking the Petfinder.com Web site. The adoption fees, adoption requirements, and adoption applications will vary, depending on the group, but most of the policies and procedures used by rescue groups are designed with the best interest of the dogs in mind.

FINDING A PET ONLINE

The Internet has created a whole new method of commerce, where business can be conducted from the comfort of your own home. When it comes to puppy buying, there are good uses of the Internet and bad uses. Purchasing a puppy from an online source without inspecting the puppy or its parents in person is never recommended. Interstate transactions can be tricky, with purchase contracts governed by the laws applicable in the breeder's state of residence. Long-distance shipping of puppies may be stressful and traumatic for the puppies. Also, it can be difficult to facilitate or enforce return, exchange, or refund policies.

The Internet does make it easy to locate dogs and puppies you would like to meet, however. Breeders and animal welfare organizations now have a wonderful medium through which to disseminate information

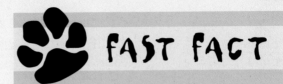

FAST FACT

Petfinder.com has an online nationwide database of adoptable dogs, which includes dogs from both shelters and rescues. A search on the Web site will locate all the Yorkshire Terriers available for adoption in your geographic area.

about adoptable dogs and announce the arrival of litters. Communicating with breeders or shelters via email is inexpensive and convenient. It would be shortsighted not to use such a wonderful tool to help locate the right dog, but precautions should be taken to avoid scams.

❧❧❧

When you choose to bring a Yorkshire Terrier into your life, you imagine all those wonderful things that come along with dog ownership—fun, companionship, loyalty, and devotion. Maybe you envision sharing your pillow with your cuddly canine or taking your portable pooch on a cross-country jaunt. Maybe you look forward to having a luxurious lap warmer on a cold winter day or partaking in the joy and laughter of watching your comic puppy play. Once you've planned the best possible beginning for your Yorkie, you can look forward to these dreams with confidence!

CHAPTER FIVE

Caring for Your Puppy (Birth to Six Months)

There is pleasure to be found in nurturing and caring for a baby Yorkie. There is pride in seeing the happiness and rambunctiousness of a healthy, well-cared-for animal. And there is a sense of accomplishment to be gained as a carefree and undisciplined pup develops into a

A Yorkshire Terrier puppy is extremely tiny, so he'll have to be handled very carefully. You'll also need to puppy-proof your home to make sure that he can't get into trouble as he grows.

well-behaved member of the household.

Your Yorkie pup is a malleable young creature that depends on you for all his needs. He needs you to protect him and make him feel safe. He needs you to teach him how to behave. He needs you to enforce consistent limits. And even when caring for him obviously seems like work—cleaning up household accidents comes to mind—everything you do contributes to the strength of your bond with your dog, because you do all these things out of love.

PUPPY-PROOFING YOUR HOME

Your heart is prepared to give a Yorkie puppy this kind of love, but are your home and your life prepared? Adding a new canine family member to your household is going to be a transition for both you and your puppy, but there are some things you can do to make these adjustments easier. Puppy-proofing your home, establishing household rules, and purchasing supplies should all be on your to-do list before acquiring your puppy.

The most important thing you can do to keep your puppy safe is to puppy-proof your home. The diminutive, inquisitive Yorkie is at risk of getting into small and dangerous places, especially when he is

such a tiny pup. Make sure any air vents at floor level are covered and access to inappropriate areas are blocked off. And don't forget that an abundance of fluffy puppy fur makes your Yorkie appear to be bigger than

Be prepared—your Yorkie puppy will get into anything and everything if you give him free run of the house.

he really is. He can squeeze through much smaller spaces than you'd think he could!

A curious, exploratory nature is known to get many a puppy into trouble. Just like human babies, puppies learn about the world by touching, tasting, and manipulating things in their environment. This puts your puppy at a high risk of choking, poisoning, or electrocution. So keep potentially dangerous houseplants, electrical cords, or small objects out of your puppy's reach. A thorough housecleaning and floor check should be conducted before you bring your Yorkie pup home.

ESTABLISHING HOUSEHOLD RULES

Deciding on household rules in advance can save you a lot of stress later. Rules and living arrangements for your puppy can be discussed with other members of your household to make sure everyone agrees on the arrangements. Besides preventing conflicts among household members, it will also contribute to consistency in your puppy's upbringing.

Where will your puppy sleep? Dogs are social animals to begin with, but puppies are especially enamored of physical closeness, since they are accustomed to the company of their mother and litter-

Your Yorkshire Terrier puppy will be happy to chew electrical cords or anything else that he can reach. Before you bring your puppy home, wires and other dangerous household items must be moved or covered so that he can't get to them.

mates. If your puppy had a say, he'd want to sleep in a crate or on a dog bed close to your own bed. Yorkies can even make good bedfellows with humans since they don't shed much hair and they don't take up much room, but if you're a heavy sleeper and worry that you might roll on top of your tiny dog and crush him, he might be safer with sleeping accommodations of his own. If you do decide to allow your Yorkie to bed down with you, keep him from becoming possessive of your bed by allowing him on the bed only when you invite him.

Deciding where your dog will eat is a lesson in practicality. Your kitchen will probably be close to the food source and have easy-to-clean flooring, but a laundry room or a dog crate may be more convenient if you need to separate your Yorkie from other pets at feeding time. No matter where you decide to feed your dog, don't be surprised if your Yorkie grabs mouthfuls of food and takes them elsewhere in the house to eat. This may be an instinctual behavior related to the way your dog's wild ancestors tore off pieces of carcass and dragged them away from the canine group to eat, thereby avoiding conflicts and competition for food.

Probably the most important decision to make is deciding where

FAST FACT

You can help your little guy adjust to his new home by enforcing your household rules from the very beginning. Although it will take a lot of repetition before your puppy learns everything he needs to know, consistency from the start will help him develop a sense of security and a close bond with you. Try to devote a lot of time to your puppy during these first critical days.

your pup will be allowed to eliminate. Choosing a specific outdoor potty area not only makes cleanup easier, it also helps in housetraining your puppy. The scents there will encourage your puppy to use the same spot every time.

You might also want to consider establishing certain limits. Do you want to limit the areas of the house where your puppy will be allowed to play until he's reliably housetrained? Do you need to limit your puppy's playtime with children so that he doesn't become overstimulated or exhausted? If there are certain indoor or outdoor areas that will be off-limits to your puppy, such as specific pieces of furniture, gardens, or hazardous areas, you are best off enforcing those limits right from the start.

PURCHASING SUPPLIES

Preparing for your new puppy isn't all serious business. Shopping for a new puppy has never been more fun. The array of pet products on the market today can take you on a journey into home decoration, fashion, and art. But regardless of how well those custom-designed food and water bowls match your décor or what kind of fashion statement that little doggy carry bag makes, there are a couple things you should always keep in mind.

First, anything you buy for your little dog should be of the appropriate size, including his collar, leash, crate, dishes, toys, and carry bag. Don't sacrifice a good fit for style. And second, all your dog's things should be washable. Anything that can be thrown into a washing machine, stacked into a dishwasher, or wiped clean with a damp cloth makes life much easier for the pet owner!

GETTING THE RIGHT STUFF

When buying supplies for your new pet, it is very easy to go overboard, spoiling your Yorkie with tons of toys and the nicest bed. However, Yorkshire Terriers don't require a lot of expensive stuff: for now, some small toys that he can chew and a basic dog bed will suffice. (Of course, if given the chance he'll happily sleep on your bed!)

You probably should spend a bit more on his food and water bowls. Purchase ceramic or metal bowls—plastic ones are cheaper, but bacteria can build up on plastic and this can lead to upset stomachs. Some dogs also chew plastic bowls apart, so you are better off investing in a good bowl right from the start.

Make sure to buy toys that are durable. No toy is indestructible, so whenever you give your Yorkie a new toy, watch him while he plays with it. If you see that the toy will come apart, take it away so that your Yorkie cannot ingest any small, sharp pieces.

If you're planning to crate-train your dog, you'll need to buy a nice plastic or wire crate. Dogs are den creatures and love having a space all their own. The crate should be big enough for your Yorkie to grow into, but not so large that he can urinate in a corner and not be bothered by the puddle. In most cases, a medium-sized crate (24 to 30 inches/61 to 76 cm) will suffice for an adult Yorkshire Terrier.

NEW PUPPY SHOPPING LIST

Collar
Leash
ID tags
Food and water bowls
Puppy food
Various chew toys

Training treats
Dog crate
Dog bed or crate pad
Doggy toothbrush and
toothpaste
Brush

Comb
Small nail clipper
Scissors
Coat or sweater
Pooper scooper

BRINGING YOUR PUPPY HOME

The exciting moment has come, and your anticipation is tempered with a bit of anxiousness. You have made all the necessary preparations, but what can you expect for the next six months? How long will it take for your puppy to adjust? What kind of development phases will your puppy go through, and how should you prepare for them?

Remember that your puppy is just a baby, and losing his mother, littermates, and the only familiar environment he's ever known is bound to be unsettling for him. Keep a large supply of patience on hand for the first few nights as your puppy adjusts to his new living situation. Your new puppy may suffer from digestive problems or diarrhea due to a change in diet, and he may become

quite vocal at night as he expresses his loneliness at having lost the company of his canine family.

You can usually avoid digestive issues associated with a change in diet by changing your puppy's diet gradually. If you know what brand of puppy food your puppy received from his breeder, feed him the same brand for a few days before changing his diet. When you're ready to introduce your puppy to a new food of your choice, do so gradually by mixing some of the new food in with the old brand over the course of several days.

Nighttime crying might be avoided by making sure your puppy receives plenty of exercise in the evening. You can't expect your puppy to sleep if he isn't tired! An active play session followed by a "settling down" period in the evening will help your pup prepare for bedtime. If he seems to be lonely in his crate, you can simulate the warmth and closeness of his littermates by wrapping a hot water bottle in a towel and putting it in his crate with him. Or, you can do what many Yorkie lovers eventually do—allow your Yorkie to snuggle on the bed with you. Just be sure that the precedent you set at this stage is one you will be happy to live with down the road.

PUPPY NUTRITION

The power of setting a precedent is most obvious when it comes to feeding practices. It only takes one tidbit from the dinner table to make a "beggar" out of a dog. It only takes a few leftovers in a dog's food bowl to create a finicky eater.

The image of many small dogs as persnickety and spoiled when it comes to their cuisine is a common one, but there's a reason for it. Small dogs have small mouths and, unlike larger dogs that tend to gulp down their food, Yorkies put a little more effort into chewing. This might explain why they tend to prefer easier-to-chew food and why taste might be a little more important to them. But it also means that Yorkie owners have to be especially diligent

To make sure your Yorkshire Terrier doesn't have trouble eating, make sure to purchase a brand of kibble specially formulated for smaller dogs. This smaller kibble will be easier for your Yorkie pup to chew.

DIETARY ALTERNATIVES

If you're willing to sacrifice the convenience of commercial dog foods, there are a couple of alternative diets you may consider for your Yorkshire Terrier. These options require the addition of dietary supplements to make them balanced and healthy, so be sure to research any alternative diet thoroughly.

Home-cooked food: The right combination of cooked meats, eggs, vegetables, cottage cheese, and other ingredients can turn people food into a healthy diet choice for dogs. While they're not considered as natural as a raw food diet, home-cooked foods do offer convenience: you can refrigerate or freeze large portions for future use.

Bones and Raw Food (B.A.R.F.): Raw meat is considered by many to be the most natural alternative diet for dogs. The B.A.R.F. diet has become so popular that commercially prepared, frozen meat patties are now widely available, but safe-handling practices must be considered when feeding your Yorkie raw meat.

in preventing feeding problems like begging and finicky eating.

Your Yorkie pup can learn to enjoy a commercial dog food diet if you stick to a smaller-size kibble, which many dog food companies produce specifically for puppies and small dogs. You can add a little bit of highly palatable canned dog food to stimulate your Yorkie's appetite without resorting to enhancing his meals with other, less healthy choices.

At this stage of his life, your puppy needs the extra calcium and vitamins provided by foods formulated especially for puppies. A good-quality puppy food will provide all the building blocks your puppy needs to develop into a healthy adult, but your puppy's health doesn't depend entirely on the type of food you feed him. It also depends on how you feed him.

It may be tempting to leave a bowl of food out at all times, especially if you have a busy schedule that makes it difficult to feed your pup at particular times, but free feeding can encourage your puppy to overeat. Worse, the lack of a regular eating schedule means your puppy's elimination patterns won't be regular. This can severely hamper your housetraining efforts. Avoid these

Introduce your Yorkie puppy to all of the people and animals in and around your home. The more you socialize your puppy, the better.

problems by feeding your puppy on a regular schedule. Give him up to 20 minutes to eat and then remove any leftover food.

COGNITIVE AND SOCIAL DEVELOPMENT

While your Yorkie puppy is growing physically, he is also growing cognitively. His little brain is learning about the rules of nature, like gravity (by falling off the couch) and mass (by running into the wall during a wild fit of play). He's learning about

grass and dirt and the warmth of sunlight. But he's also learning social skills and gaining self-confidence.

Be sure to provide as many positive social experiences as possible for your young dog, because puppies that don't learn social skills at a young age may not be able to learn them as adults. Studies have shown that puppies can become fearful of things to which they have not been adequately exposed by the time they are 12 weeks old. Not only is it crucial to expose your puppy to as many different people, animals, and objects as possible, it's just as important to make sure these encounters are pleasant. A bad experience for your puppy at this age could create a life-long phobia.

Your puppy needs to learn that other dogs are good. He needs to learn that children are good, and men with hats are good, and that vacuum cleaners won't eat him. If you have no children of your own, you can invite some neighborhood children to play with your puppy occasionally—under supervision, of course. You should take your young Yorkie for plenty of walks so he can see the world from his own four feet and develop trust and confidence in the world around him. Be sure to stop and chat with your neighbors, too, as these are great social opportunities! You can even arrange play-dates for your Yorkie with other small dogs in the neighborhood, so your Yorkie can learn proper canine social skills as well.

GROOMING YOUR YORKIE'S COAT

Socializing your Yorkie is a great excuse to show off your new pup! You can double your pride if your pup is clean and well groomed. Even if your puppy hasn't quite grown into the luxurious length of hair of an adult Yorkie, you might as well prepare for it by getting your pup accustomed to regular brushing and combing while his coat is still short and manageable.

Grooming is not an option for Yorkshire Terriers; it's a necessity. Ask any woman with long hair how much care she must put into it and you'll get a pretty good idea of the kind of care a Yorkie's coat demands. You can cut back on some of the time required to maintain your dog's coat by using the services of a professional dog groomer. A groomer can help with the maintenance of a full coat, or she can keep your dog's coat trimmed short. She can also take care of other hygiene items like

FAST FACT

The best way to remove tangles from long hair is to start brushing the ends of the hair first, and then work your way closer to the skin. You can avoid pulling on your dog's skin by holding the hair close to the skin with your free hand while brushing the ends of the hair. Shorter hair can be held in a scissors grip between your index finger and middle finger while brushing. Use detanglers on problem areas, always remove all mats and tangles before a bath, and apply a conditioner during the bath to keep your Yorkie's hair in the best condition.

A slicker brush will help you keep your Yorkshire Terrier looking his best.

baths, nail trimmings, and ear cleanings. Many Yorkie lovers find that bringing their dog to a professional dog groomer every six to eight weeks simplifies their lives considerably.

Even so, be prepared to do some maintenance brushing in between groomer visits. This will help keep your dog's hair in good condition in the interim, and it will also provide bonding opportunities for you and your dog.

After a good brushing, you can use a comb to part your dog's hair from the base of his head to the end of his tail, and then comb his hair down each side of his body to give him the distinctive Yorkie "do." If it's long enough, the hair on your dog's snout should also be parted down the middle. The hair on the top of his head can be parted to fall down each side of his head, or it can be drawn up into a topknot. This is the part of your Yorkie that can be personalized according to your own taste.

The topknot can be held in place by a small rubber band and then dressed up by affixing a bow. Red bows have become standard apparel for Yorkies in the show ring, but your Yorkie can don any type of bow you'd like. Red bows with white polka dots are exceptionally striking for informal outings, glittery bows are quite catchy for formal affairs, and specialty bows with holiday patterns are popular for Halloween, Christmas, and other occasions!

Until your Yorkie pup gets used to a topknot, though, use rubber bands only. You don't want your puppy to pull out a bow and chew or choke on it. And when you need to remove the topknot, cut the rubber band carefully with a scissors. Attempting to pull the rubber band out will tear the hair and cause your dog unnecessary discomfort. Tiny rubber bands are inexpensive and can be purchased in large quantities any place hair accessories are sold.

BATHING

Yorkies make great couch companions during the day and pillow puppies at night. The importance of cleanliness for your Yorkie becomes obvious when you consider the close spaces you share with him.

Fortunately, the Yorkie's small size proves to have yet another advantage: He can easily fit in the kitchen sink for baths.

A rubber mat to prevent slipping and a spray nozzle are must-haves to accomplish this task. Just be sure to assemble your bathing supplies ahead of time so you won't have to abandon your dripping-wet dog in the sink to go look for them. Shampoo, conditioner, a towel, and cotton balls to keep water out of your dog's ears should all be within arm's reach of the sink.

There are a few rules you must abide by when bathing a long-haired dog. First, make sure you have brushed your dog and removed all the tangles and mats before getting him wet. Tangles and mats will become even tighter and more difficult to remove after they become wet. Use a detangling product, if necessary.

Second, be sure to rinse the hair thoroughly after shampooing and conditioning. It's difficult to get all the shampoo and conditioner out of a long coat. Shampoo left in the coat

After your Yorkie is finished with his bath, be sure to dry him thoroughly. You can wrap him in a towel to keep him warm and remove most of the moisture, but for best results use an electric hair dryer set to the lowest heat level.

can dry out your dog's skin and leave his coat dull and hard to manage. Too much conditioner left in the coat may make the coat waxy and limp. So even when you think you've rinsed your dog's coat well enough, rinse it a couple more times just to be sure.

Third, long hair takes a long time to dry, especially the hair close to the skin. If you keep your Yorkie trimmed short, you can get away with allowing him to air dry, but if your Yorkie has a long coat, you'll have to use a hair dryer to dry him. It's not healthy for your dog's skin, coat, or general health to leave him wet for long periods. A human hair dryer on a low heat setting will work just fine, but be patient with your little Yorkie as he learns to feel comfortable with it.

NAIL CARE

Nail clipping is best done immediately after a bath, when your dog's nails are soft and easy to trim. Your puppy may not appreciate this procedure much, but he will learn to tolerate it quite well if it's performed regularly. If you're nervous about trimming your puppy's nails, you can give this responsibility to your veterinarian or a professional groomer, who will do it for a modest fee. When your puppy has learned to be

more tolerant, you may gain the confidence to do it yourself. In either case, your puppy will need to have his nails clipped every two to four weeks, depending on how fast his nails grow.

You can purchase a nail clipper that is the appropriate size for your Yorkie at any pet supply store. To trim his nails, hold the blades of the clipper perpendicular to the nail and then clip off the tip. Be careful not to trim the nail too short, as you may cut into the quick, which provides the nail's blood supply. This can cause pain and bleeding that your puppy is not likely to soon forget. You can avoid cutting the quick by looking at the nail from the side to determine how much nail is excess growth. Better to leave the nails a little longer than necessary and trim them more frequently than to give your dog—and you—a bad nail clipping experience.

EAR CARE

The tips of the Yorkshire Terrier's ears are customarily shaved and trimmed along the edges to give them a sharp, alert presence atop the Yorkie's head. Erect ears thus groomed have a relatively low chance of ear infection, as plenty of air circulation helps to keep the ear canals dry. If your dog does show irritation of the ears by shaking his head, scratching his ears, walking in circles or losing his balance, it's time to see your veterinarian.

Preventing moisture from getting into your dog's ears by placing cotton balls in them prior to bathing is a good practice. You can further contribute to your dog's good ear health by gently wiping the ears out once a week with a cotton ball moistened with isopropyl alcohol (rubbing alcohol). The alcohol will help kill any bacteria, and it will also act as a drying agent.

DENTAL CARE

Your Yorkie's preference for softer, easier-to-chew food has drawbacks other than the risk of finicky eating habits. It also puts your Yorkie at risk of dental problems. Soft foods tend to stick to the teeth and form tartar. The tartar eventually hardens into bacteria-laden plaque along the gum line,

which can cause serious periodontal disease.

To make matters worse, small dogs are not known to be heavy chewers. Providing dental chews will probably not be enough to encourage your dog to keep his teeth clean on his own. Oral health is something your little dog will definitely need your help with. Since periodontal disease can cause significant pain, loss of teeth, and possibly lead to serious infections, brushing your dog's teeth once a week or more will do much more than provide your dog with a sparkling smile and fresh breath.

Getting started is quite easy. Dental kits for dogs are now readily available at most pet supply stores, and specially flavored doggy

Take good care of your Yorkie's teeth. Dental problems can lead to other health issues, such as heart disease.

toothpastes are designed to make tooth brushing a pleasurable experience for your dog. Just like any other part of his grooming routine, your dog will learn to tolerate the handling of his mouth if you introduce him to it gradually. In addition, you should make sure your dog receives a complete oral checkup from your veterinarian each year.

TRAINING

Whether your puppy is destined for the prestige of a championship or if he will simply become the king of your lap, he needs to be trained. It's not easy to live with any type of canine, even a small one, if there are no limits to his behavior. The first orders of business when it comes to training puppies under six months old are establishing rules of behavior, crate training, and housetraining.

The sooner you discourage behaviors like jumping on your legs, nipping at your hands, or chewing on inappropriate items, the easier it will be to get your puppy to stop these behaviors. If you allow these behaviors to persist, they will become deeply ingrained habits. Jumping and nipping are best dealt with by issuing a firm "No!" or "Uh-uh!" and then redirecting your puppy to a more appropriate activity. If your persistent pup refuses to desist, the worst consequence you can give him is to withhold your attention until he calms down.

Chewing is also a common problem with puppies, but a little understanding is in order. It is a very natural and necessary part of your puppy's development for him to explore with his mouth, and the teething phase between two and six months of age further spurs your puppy into chewing on anything he can sink his teeth into. Be sure to provide your pup with plenty of appropriate chew toys of different sizes, textures, and shapes that will entice him. Issue a firm "No!" if you catch your pup chewing on anything inappropriate and immediately replace the item with one of your puppy's toys. Many chewing conflicts can be avoided simply by keeping your puppy confined to

Make sure that your Yorkie has appropriate toys to chew, so that he won't be tempted to gnaw on your shoes.

CRATING DOS AND DON'TS

Don't confine your puppy for periods longer than one hour for every month of his age. Puppies can't be expected to have bowel or bladder control for periods longer than that, and you don't want your puppy to get in the habit of eliminating in his crate.

Do provide your puppy with a larger area of confinement, with an appropriate elimination area, if you need to confine your puppy for longer periods.

Don't rush crate training. Take your time, be patient, and don't push your puppy any faster than his comfort level will allow.

Do provide comfortable bedding and toys in the crate. The more comfortable you make it, the more your puppy will love to spend time in his crate.

Don't use a crate for punishment. This will make your puppy learn to fear his crate.

Do use a crate whenever you take your puppy in a vehicle. Not only is this a safe way for your puppy to travel, but he'll also learn to associate his crate with the excitement of travel.

safe areas and keeping temptations out of your puppy's reach.

CRATE TRAINING

One of the easiest ways to manage your puppy's behavior is to keep your puppy in a crate when you can't supervise him. Confining your puppy to a crate can help prevent chewing damage and housetraining lapses. It's also a safe way to transport your puppy while traveling on vacation, to shows, or to the vet's office. But using a crate can be frustrating and annoying if you have to listen to your puppy fuss and carry on whenever he is crated, especially if it causes you to lose sleep at night.

You can teach your puppy to accept his crate without all the drama. If you allow your puppy regular access to his crate and continually encourage him to use it by putting treats and toys in it, he will begin to regard it as his own safe place. As your puppy starts to use his crate voluntarily, you can begin to close the door to the crate for very short periods. Be sure to give your puppy something to keep him busy in his crate, like a consumable chew item, to discourage any fussing. As your puppy's comfort level rises, you can gradually increase the amount of time you keep your puppy confined, but this should not exceed one hour for every month of your puppy's age (i.e., a three-month-old puppy should not be confined more than three hours, a five-month-old puppy should not be confined more than five hours, and so on).

A crate is a very useful tool for puppy-rearing, but it should not be abused. No puppy or dog should be confined to a crate for more than six hours. If you need to confine your puppy for longer periods, find a safe room or set up a puppy pen. You want your puppy to associate his crate with only good things, so make it as comfortable as possible for him and never use it for punishment.

HOUSETRAINING

Housetraining can be the most frustrating training issue for puppy owners. No one likes the thought of cleaning up accidents in the home, so it's always been a priority to get a puppy housetrained as quickly as possible, using whatever methods might work. The problem is that housetraining is not always a quick process, especially for small dogs, and traditional methods of swatting a

dog with a rolled-up newspaper or pushing his nose into his own feces are more traumatic than effective.

You can avoid much of the frustration of housetraining if you have realistic expectations, manage your puppy in a way that minimizes accidents,

Housetraining a dog can be very frustrating, but be patient. With time and practice, your Yorkie will understand that he has to "do his business" outside—every time.

and use techniques that really work. First, you should be aware that it does tend to take longer to housetrain small dogs, like Yorkshire Terriers. There are a number of theories as to why this is, including speculation that small dogs mature mentally at a later age than larger dogs and that the spatial perception of small dogs is different from that of larger dogs (for a Yorkie, going across the room to eliminate is the same as going out into the yard for a larger dog). The important thing for you to realize, however, is that it may take up to a year for your Yorkie to become reliably housetrained.

Until then, you can minimize accidents by following various management practices. Keep your puppy on a regular feeding and exercise schedule to help regulate his elimination patterns. Take your puppy to his outdoor area at times when he is most likely to go, such as after eating or upon waking. Restrict your dog's space in the house and supervise him closely when he's outside his confinement areas. Learn to recognize the signals your dog gives when he needs to go, such as circling while sniffing the floor or sniffing the floor with a hunched back.

Punishment after an accident has never been, and will never be, effective. It only serves to make a puppy fearful, as he is not capable of understanding what he has done wrong after the fact. You can, however, take advantage of the occasions when you actually catch your puppy in the act of elimination. Scoop up your puppy quickly and take him promptly to his outdoor spot. Plenty of praise each time your puppy gets it right will encourage him to use the appropriate area in the future.

CHAPTER SIX

Your Yorkie's Health

As a pet owner, you're responsible for making sure that your Yorkshire Terrier is in good health. It's important to find a veterinarian you can trust, and to understand the potential health issues common to dogs of this breed.

Once you've found the perfect Yorkie, one of your first duties will be to have your new pet examined by a veterinarian. A veterinary exam can detect any preexisting conditions that may affect the future health of your dog. You'll also be introducing your pet to the vet that he will be seeing on a regular basis. It is important for the three of you to develop a good rapport.

Regular exercise is a requirement for your Yorkie to stay healthy and happy.

CHOOSING A VETERINARIAN

There are two steps in evaluating a veterinary clinic—a telephone inquiry and an in-person visit. You can begin evaluating veterinary clinics by phone even before acquiring your new dog. Ask about the facilities and equipment the clinic has to offer, as well as about the price of various procedures. If a clinic does not have its own lab testing, x-ray, or ultrasound equipment, expect to be referred to other facilities for these services. If the clinic's hours of operation conflict with your work schedule, you'll find it difficult to get there when you need to. And if the clinic is located a considerable distance from your home, it may mean the loss of critical minutes in getting emergency care for your dog. Take all these factors into consideration when conducting your telephone interviews.

After you've completed your research by phone, the next step is to meet the vet at the top of your list. The most convenient time to evaluate the clinic you've chosen in

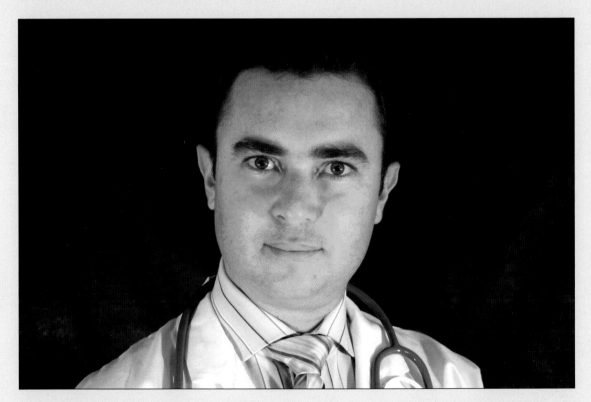

When looking for a veterinarian, seek recommendations from your pet-owning friends or family members. Ask them what it is they like about their vet. Then, meet the vet and check out his clinic yourself.

AAHA ®
AMERICAN ANIMAL HOSPITAL ASSOCIATION

Healthy Practices.
Healthier Pets.

When interviewing a prospective vet, ask if his or her clinic is a member of the American Animal Hospital Association. Clinics that are accredited by AAHA are inspected regularly, and must adhere to the organization's standards for cleanliness and care.

person is during your dog's initial routine veterinary exam. This is a great opportunity to observe exactly how your dog is treated and get a firsthand feel for the service you can expect if more serious medical issues should arise in the future. It is important to choose a veterinarian you can trust, and, for most people, this means finding a vet who has the right combination of intelligence,

compassion, and understanding. Your veterinarian should listen to your concerns and take the time to answer your questions in terms you can understand. And, of course, she should treat your dog with the utmost kindness.

Evaluating the clinic staff can be just as important as evaluating the veterinarian. It doesn't do much good to find an outstanding vet if the clinic staff is lazy, incompetent, or treats your dog like a lab rat rather than the cherished family companion that he is. Be extremely observant on your first visit. Your vet's job is to examine your dog; your job is to examine your vet.

THE VETERINARY EXAM

Be prepared for your Yorkie's first veterinary exam by bringing along any medical records supplied by your dog's breeder or adoption organization, and don't forget to write down any questions you may have concerning your dog's health, development, or behavior. Your vet may also request that you bring a stool sample to be tested for internal parasites. As tempting as it may be to "accidentally" forget to perform this odious chore, it's a vital part of evaluating your little dog's health.

Your Yorkie's initial exam should be a thorough one. Your vet should check your Yorkie's eyes, ears, nose, and mouth. Your dog's abdomen should be palpated to feel for any abnormalities. Your dog's heart and lungs should be checked with a stethoscope, and his coat and skin condition should be noted. A veterinarian who also manipulates your Yorkie's rear legs to check for any sign of knee problems, which are common in small dogs, is doing an exemplary job.

PARASITES

A very important function of the veterinary exam is to detect the presence of external or internal parasites.

Your dog's skin and coat condition can signal the presence of external parasites, and the aforementioned stool sample can reveal the presence of internal parasites. A blood test can further determine if your dog has been infected with heartworms. Since almost all dogs are infected by parasites at some time during their lives, it doesn't hurt to add the symptoms they cause to your bank of knowledge.

EXTERNAL PARASITES: The most common and annoying external parasite for dogs is the flea, which can survive almost anywhere in North

CANINE FIRST AID

When a dog joins your family, it's important to have canine first aid supplies on hand. Your canine first aid kit should contain the following items:

- gauze pads
- antibiotic ointment
- hydrogen peroxide
- petroleum jelly
- eye wash
- ear wash
- medications
- sterile stretch gauze
- bandage scissors

- splints
- a blanket
- tweezers
- tensor bandage
- copies of the dog's health records (such as CERF or OFA certification and other paperwork)

- bismuth tablets
- rectal thermometer
- medications
- local and national poison control numbers
- phone numbers for your regular veterinary clinic and the emergency clinic.

America. Even though they prefer warmer climates and tend to reproduce seasonally, fleas can thrive and reproduce year-round in the cozy confines of your home. They are particularly irritating to dogs, as they cause incessant itching and scratching that can lead to skin sores and infections. Dogs that are allergic to flea saliva can succumb to a severe rash, called flea bite dermatitis. But worse than that, fleas serve as intermediary hosts for tapeworm larvae, which are easily passed on to your dog.

Besides the obvious discomfort indicated by scratching and biting, you can tell if your dog has fleas by running your fingers through his hair and looking for small brown insects

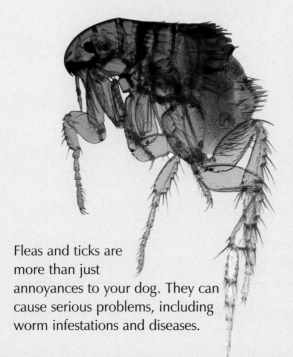

Fleas and ticks are more than just annoyances to your dog. They can cause serious problems, including worm infestations and diseases.

scurrying along his skin or the tiny black droppings, called flea dirt, they leave behind. A bath with an insecticidal shampoo or rinse will quickly eradicate these pests from your dog, but you will also have to treat indoor and outdoor areas of your home with the appropriate insecticidal products. Then, a couple weeks later, you'll have to treat your dog and his environment again to kill off any emerging fleas that were not wiped out by the first treatment.

Another external parasite, the tick, doesn't cause such obvious discomfort, but it is no less threatening to your dog's health. Ticks are known to transmit a number of potentially devastating diseases to both dogs and humans, including the dreaded Lyme disease. Ticks are small, flat parasites that burrow their tiny heads into their host's skin to subsist on blood. They are particularly attracted to the blood-rich skin of a dog's ears and face.

If you find a tick on your dog, it should be removed as quickly as possible by grasping the tick close to the head with tweezers, then pulling it off. The longer a tick remains embedded in your dog's skin, the greater the chance it will transmit a tick-borne disease to your dog.

Dealing with external parasites is no fun. If you live in an area where fleas or ticks are prevalent, you might want to consider avoiding these pests altogether by using a preventative. Spot treatments and flea collars can help repel these bothersome creatures.

INTERNAL PARASITES: Internal parasites may be hidden from view, but their symptoms are not. A bloated belly, a lackluster coat, an itchy rear end, and a loss of energy are all signs of intestinal worms, which include roundworms, hookworms, whipworms, and tapeworms. Intestinal worms are extremely common in puppies; some of them can be transmitted to the pups even before they are born. As if this weren't enough to guarantee an infection, worms can also be transmitted to newborn puppies through their mother's milk or acquired from the environment.

The most devastating of all internal parasites is heartworm, which is spread by mosquitoes and develops in the dog's circulatory system. This parasite can cause poor general health, as well as an obvious lack of energy and difficulty breathing during

CANINE TICK-BORNE DISEASES

Lyme disease: Causes various degrees of joint swelling, arthritis, fevers, and fatigue.

Ehrlichiosis: Symptoms include anemia, high fever, and lethargy.

Tick paralysis: Characterized by a lack of coordination of the rear limbs, which may progress to complete paralysis of the rear legs.

Rocky Mountain spotted fever: Obviously causes a fever, but is also known to cause loss of appetite, vomiting, diarrhea, muscle and joint aches, anemia, and neurological symptoms, such as dizziness and seizures.

Babesiosis: Known to cause fever, anemia, weakness, depression, dehydration, and shock.

exercise. What makes these parasites so horrific is the permanent damage they can cause to the heart and lungs, and the risky treatment required to kill them.

A poison must be injected into the dog to eradicate the heartworms, but the poison is also toxic to the dog and can cause serious health complications. Another danger is that a large number of dead heartworms could cause blockages in the dog's system. Due to these risks and the fact that heartworm continues to spread geographically, it's highly advisable to have your Yorkie tested

THE DANGER OF HEARTWORMS

Heartworms are a concern for all dog owners. The graphic above illustrates the cycle of heartworm development. When a mosquito (1) bites a Yorkie, it can inject microfilaria into his bloodstream. The microfilaria travel through the bloodstream to the heart (2), where they grow into heartworms (3) and multiply, clogging the dog's heart. If left untreated, heartworms can kill.

FAST FACT

Dogs should be checked for internal parasites at least once a year. Take a small fecal sample to your veterinarian and have it examined for microscopic worm eggs.

annually for heartworm and keep him on a monthly preventative.

VACCINATIONS

Preventing health problems is one of the most important functions of veterinary medicine, and the most common form of prevention is vaccination. The purpose of vaccinating your dog against various diseases goes beyond preventing your dog from suffering. Vaccinations prevent dogs from spreading diseases among themselves or transmitting diseases to humans.

Having your dog vaccinated is as much a civic duty as it is a way to keep your Yorkie healthy. Puppies should receive a series of puppy vaccinations to help their little bodies develop the immunities they need. For adult dogs, most vaccines are now given in three-year intervals. Don't worry about your poor pup becoming a canine pincushion— vaccines for many of the following diseases are available in combination doses, so your pup doesn't have to get a separate injection for each one.

DISTEMPER: Canine distemper is a virus that can be spread in many ways—through the air or by contact with an infected dog's feces, urine, or things he may have touched. It affects the nervous system and causes symptoms ranging from lethargy and fever to vomiting and diarrhea. This illness is often distinguished from other canine viruses by the eye and nasal discharge it causes. Distemper must not be taken lightly. This virus is fatal to a majority of puppies and half the adult dogs that become infected with it.

Like most viruses, there is no cure for distemper. Treatment is limited to supportive care in the form of intravenous (IV) fluids and medications to treat the symptoms. The highly contagious nature and devastating effects of this virus make prevention a priority.

PARVOVIRUS: Canine parvovirus is spread through an infected dog's secretions and is highly contagious. This is a serious gastrointestinal disease that can also affect the heart and blood cells. Symptoms of this virus include lethargy, fevers, vomiting, and bloody diarrhea. Treatment is limited to supportive care, but even with the best efforts, it often results in death for puppies. Fortunately, the incidence of parvo infection among dogs has decreased dramatically since the development of a vaccine, and you can do your part to keep this disease out of the canine population by vaccinating your puppy against this virus.

CORONAVIRUS: Another gastro-intestinal disease that upsets the digestive system, with vomiting and diarrhea, is canine coronavirus. This disease is spread by contact with an infected dog or its feces. The effect on a dog can range from asympto-matic to serious, depending on the individual. A vaccine is available to provide protection for dogs and peace of mind for dog owners.

PARAINFLUENZA: Canine para-influenza is a respiratory illness similar to the human cold virus. It is spread through the air and through secretions, and it causes coughing, a nasal discharge, and bronchial inflammation. Even though it is not generally considered serious, parain-fluenza can make your dog miserable and can lead to other conditions such as kennel cough or pneumonia.

INFECTIOUS CANINE HEPATITIS: Formally called canine adenovirus-1,

Following your vet's vaccination protocol for your Yorkie will help to ensure that your best friend will be around to share the good times for many years.

infectious canine hepatitis is a virus that targets a dog's liver and kidneys. It is often spread through the air, but can also be ingested by the dog. Symptoms can range from mild fever and lethargy to jaundice, shock, and death. The potential seriousness of this disease is enough to put it on the list of "must-haves" among canine vaccinations.

KENNEL COUGH: Kennel cough, also known as bordetella, is responsible for a highly contagious respiratory condition that causes a chronic dry cough and bronchial inflammation. Although the bacterium *Bordetella bronchiseptica* is the primary perpetrator, it's not the only one. Kennel cough is believed to be caused by a combination of the Bordetella bacteria and viruses like canine parainfluenza and canine adenovirus-2. A nasal vaccine against bordetella in combination with the vaccines against the other two viruses, effectively protects a dog from kennel cough.

Since the condition is not considered serious and it tends to be a problem only in situations where it can be spread among a group of dogs, bordetella vaccine is not a necessity for all dogs. But if you plan to take obedience lessons, show your dog, or even take your dog to the dog park where other dogs congregate, it's definitely recommended.

LEPTOSPIROSIS: Leptospirosis is a bacterial infection for which vaccination may only be necessary in areas where an outbreak has occurred. This disease is spread through the urine of

VACCINATION SCHEDULE FOR PUPPIES

The following vaccination schedule is recommended by the American Animal Hospital Association:

Vaccine	Age of Puppy
Distemper	8 weeks and 12 weeks
Parvovirus	8 weeks, 12 weeks, 16 weeks
Parainfluenza	8 weeks, 12 weeks
Coronavirus	8 weeks, 12 weeks
Canine adenovirus-2	8 weeks, 12 weeks
Leptospirosis	8 weeks, 12 weeks
Bordetella*	12 weeks
Lyme disease*	12 weeks, 16 weeks
Rabies +	16 weeks

* Optional vaccines, depending on location and risk.   + Required by law.
Source: American Animal Hospital Association

If you live in an area where deer are plentiful, your veterinarian may recommend vaccinating your dog against Lyme disease, as this debilitating disease is carried by deer ticks.

infected animals and affects the kidneys and liver. Symptoms may include lethargy, kidney inflammation, jaundice, and excessive consumption of water. Antibiotics can effectively treat this disease.

LYME DISEASE: Lyme disease is transmitted by ticks and causes varying degrees of symptoms. Infected dogs may experience joint stiffness and swelling similar to arthritis. Fever and lethargy are also common symptoms. Vaccination is recommended in areas where ticks are a problem.

RABIES: Finally, we come to the bad boy of all viral infections: rabies. With a list of terrifying symptoms that include delirium, unprovoked aggression, and the inability to swallow (causing the drooling or "frothing at the mouth" most commonly associated with an infected dog), rabies is a terribly frightening disease. It is always fatal and can be transmitted to people. For this reason, state laws require the vaccination of all dogs against rabies. Thanks to such strict controls, the transmission of rabies from dogs to humans is now extremely rare, and the incidence of rabies among dogs has declined substantially.

COMMON HEALTH PROBLEMS

Your veterinarian is instrumental in getting your dog off to a good, healthy start with an examination and vaccinations, but your dog's future health also depends a lot on you. How do you know when your dog requires veterinary attention? Would you know how to recognize common canine health problems or hereditary problems that affect Yorkshire Terriers? The more you know, the better you will be able to determine when veterinary care is necessary.

EYE DISORDERS: Yorkshire Terriers are prone to a number of hereditary eye disorders that can result in excessive tearing, squinting, pawing at the eyes, or other signs of eye irritation. Distichiasis is a condition in which abnormally growing eyelashes can abrade the eye, and entropion is a defect that causes the eyelids to roll inward and cause irritation. Both conditions can be resolved with surgery.

More serious eye conditions can cause partial or total blindness. The most common of these are cataracts and progressive retinal atrophy. Cataracts are characterized by opaque obstructions in the lens of the eye. The lens can be surgically replaced by an artificial lens to restore full vision. Progressive retinal atrophy, however, does not have such a promising prognosis, as there is no cure and total blindness is inevitable. If you see any sign of eye irritation or loss of vision, consult your veterinarian immediately.

ORTHOPEDIC DISORDERS: Your Yorkie's diminutive size is one of his most appealing characteristics, but it also puts him at risk of a common orthopedic disorder associated with many small dogs: patellar luxation. This condition involves a kneecap that slips out of place; the severity of which determines how painful it can be and what treatment to administer.

FAST FACT

Jeanna Giese of Fond du Lac, Wisconsin, was the first and only person ever known to have survived rabies without being vaccinated prior to the onset of symptoms. To date, attempts to duplicate the treatment she received have not resulted in the survival of any other human rabies patient. One anomaly does not change the status of rabies. It is still considered a fatal disease.

Some dogs are mildly affected, with a kneecap that pops back into place on its own, while other dogs exhibit chronic pain by limping or skipping with their back legs. Consult your veterinarian to find out how to best treat your dog.

Less common, but still a concern for Yorkshire Terriers, is Legg-Calve-Perthes disease, which affects the ball-and-socket joint of the hip. In dogs with this disease, the ball part of this joint, at the end of the femur bone, deteriorates due to poor blood supply. This eventually affects the performance of the joint and causes pain. Surgery is a viable treatment option for this condition as well.

SKIN DISORDERS: Poor skin and coat condition, or a loss of hair that cannot be attributed to poor diet, fleas, or other obvious causes, may be related to a hereditary condition. Young Yorkshire Terriers that suffer from patchy hair loss may be affected by demodicosis, a form of mange. A certain number of demodex mites normally live within the layers of a dog's skin, but the dog's immune system keeps the population of mites in check. An immunodeficiency syndrome that is believed to be hereditary allows demodex mites to reproduce unchecked and causes patchy hair loss. Fortunately, the condition can be treated and is often outgrown as the dog matures and develops better immunity.

Seborrhea is another skin condition that affects Yorkies. It causes excess production of sebum (skin oil) and can result in scaly skin. Paying particular attention to hygiene, with frequent baths and grooming, is the only way to treat this condition.

Hereditary eye disorders like distichiasis, entropion, and cataracts are common among Yorkshire Terriers. If you see signs that your Yorkie's eyes may be irritated, have his vision checked immediately.

HEREDITARY DISEASES

Other hereditary diseases associated with Yorkshire Terriers include the following:

Hepatic porto systemic shunt: Abnormal blood vessels in the liver

Hydrocephalus: Accumulation of fluid in the brain

Hypoplasia of dens: Improper development of the second vertebra

Keratitis sicca: Insufficient production of tears in one or both eyes

Patent ductus arteriosus: Improper development of the vessel connecting the aorta and pulmonary artery

Persistent papillary membrane: Improper development of the iris membrane of the eye

Retinal detachment: The retina is not attached to the back of the eye

Retinal dysplasia: A malformed retina

von Willebrand's disease: A bleeding disorder that prevents proper clotting of the blood

ENDOCRINE DISORDERS: The endocrine system is responsible for maintaining the correct balance of hormones and enzymes so that all the other systems of the body can operate properly. Cushing's disease, also known as hyperadrenocorticism, is an endocrine disorder caused by a pituitary or adrenal gland tumor. The disruption in hormone balance can result in symptoms ranging from hair loss and skin infections to a bloating in the abdomen. While an adrenal gland tumor may be surgically removed, there is no cure for a pituitary tumor. In this case, the disease must be managed with medication.

Hypothyroidism is another condition that disrupts the endocrine system. This common problem afflicts more than 50 dog breeds, including the Yorkie. If a dog has this condition, his own immune system targets the thyroid gland, causing insufficient production of hormones. This can result in a variety of symptoms, such as hair loss, skin conditions, and a loss of energy. The good news is that this condition is easily treated with an inexpensive, daily hormone supplement.

CHAPTER SEVEN

Things to Know as Your Puppy Grows

By the time your Yorkshire puppy is six months old, he has almost reached his adult height. But don't let this fool you. He'll be growing physically and mentally up through the age of two years. His joints are still forming, his muscles are still developing, and his brain is still going through typical developmental stages. You may even have noticed some changes in your Yorkie's behavior around this time.

It can be a lot of fun to pamper your growing Yorkie pup, adorning her with colorful bows for others to admire and enjoy.

COGNITIVE DEVELOPMENT

Your Yorkie may appear to suffer from a split personality at times. Perhaps your Yorkie doesn't listen to you as well as he used to, or, worse, he purposely ignores you. Maybe he's decided to test the tolerance of other pets in the household and has started to cause conflicts with them. And then, just when you think you need to consult a doggy shrink, your pup becomes as sweet and compliant as a dutiful canine companion should be. This Jekyll and Hyde personality is often equated with the teenage years in human children.

Your puppy has entered a defiant stage when he tests the limits of how much control he has and where he fits within the social hierarchy. During this time, you must be firm and consistent with your Yorkie. Your little dog will eventually outgrow this phase, but how you handle your dog at this stage can have a lasting impact on his behavior.

Small dogs easily earn the reputation of being nippy and possessive when such "teenage" behavior is allowed to go unchecked. It may seem cute when such a little dog

As he grows, expect your Yorkie to test you by refusing to acknowledge your commands. If you firmly insist on obedience, he'll eventually come back around.

displays ridiculously disproportionate bravado, but there is nothing cute about it. Be sure to enforce strict limits on your puppy's behavior during this critical growth period.

PHYSICAL GROWTH

Yorkshire Terriers have a lot in common with other toy dogs, including the fact that they stop growing much earlier than larger dogs. This may be because they just don't have as much growing to do, or it may be due to the gene that controls a dog's size. Regardless, it may be preferable to switch your Yorkie to an adult dog

food at 10 months old to prevent too much weight gain from the higher-calorie puppy food.

Slow growth does not mean stagnant growth. Your puppy's immature bone structure and joints are still subject to injury under stress. Joint damage to a young dog is not easily repaired. If you're interested in participating in a physically demanding activity with your Yorkie, like an Agility competition, you should closely monitor your puppy's exercise regimen to avoid injuries.

As in all things, going to one extreme or the other is not healthy. A lack of exercise can be just as damaging as too much exercise. Make sure your puppy engages in a balanced program of low-energy exercise, like walking, as well as aerobic exercise, such as a good game of fetch, every day.

NUTRITION

Another crucial component of your dog's development is nutrition, which doesn't always get the attention it deserves. Dry commercial dog foods all pretty much look the same—they're dry, crunchy, kibbled, and mostly brown. But if you care about your Yorkie's health, you need to read the fine print on the packages.

A quality dog food will have a tremendous effect on your dog's appearance and attitude. If you want to see how shiny and silky your Yorkie's coat can be, and how much sparkle can light up his eyes, choose a dog food that uses quality ingredients. The first few ingredients listed on the package should be pure meat products like turkey or chicken, rather than meat by-products or grain meals.

Much concern has been raised about the safety of additives used to preserve freshness, add color, or enhance the flavor of commercial dog foods. Quality foods now use vitamin E as a natural preservative.

Like most dogs, Yorkshire Terriers enjoy gnawing on a bone or rawhide chew from time to time. However, your Yorkie should be supervised when he's chewing one of these treats. Some dogs can break them apart and choke on the pieces.

Those fancy-colored kibbles are designed to appeal to humans, not to dogs, so that boring brown color may actually be the healthier choice.

Your little dog will no doubt show a preference for the more palatable semi-moist kibble and other soft foods, but you should pay attention to what you're really feeding your dog. As much as your dog may like them, moist foods tend to be loaded with salt and preservatives. A quality canned food is a better choice, but keep in mind that canned foods contain up to 90 percent moisture and do not contain as much actual food for the price. That's why a compromise of mixing some canned food with dry food is a good option.

Now that your puppy is not growing as rapidly as he did before, he

You can tell if your Yorkie is getting a little too chunky by feeling his ribs. You should be able to feel your dog's ribs through a moderate layer of tissue, which is an indication that he is at his optimum weight. If you can feel your dog's ribs easily, he could probably use a little more kibble at mealtime. If you have a lot of difficulty feeling the individual ribs, you may need to cut back his food intake and take him for an extra daily walk.

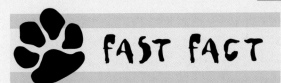

If your young Yorkie appears to be packing on a few extra ounces, reduce the amount you feed him and increase his exercise in small increments until his weight returns to a healthy level. Avoid low-calorie dog foods, however, as these are also low in protein, which your young dog needs for proper physical development. Low-calorie dog foods should be used only at the recommendation of a veterinarian.

can no longer benefit from extra calories. He'll just get fat. So at this point you have to become more careful about how much you feed your dog, as one extra pound (0.5 kg) of weight on a five-pound (2.3 kg) Yorkie is sure to be noticeable. If you measure your dog's food and check his weight occasionally, you can adjust the amount you feed him accordingly.

HEALTH ISSUES

Your puppy's good health depends on a good diet, but it also depends on the ongoing health care you provide. Your puppy has been developing immunities to many serious diseases during his first year, thanks to the series of vaccinations he received in the first few months of his life. But these immunities are still not fully developed. He will need one more set of booster vaccinations at one year old before it will be safe to put him on the three-year vaccination schedule used for adult dogs.

Annual veterinary checkups should be an important part of your Yorkie's health care regimen throughout his life, even when he is not due for vaccinations. Dental issues are always a concern for Yorkies, and annual heartworm tests have become vitally important.

Many hereditary problems tend to present themselves within the first two years of a dog's life, so you should be on the lookout for any unusual symptoms. Any sign of eye problems, digestive problems, or neurological problems should be brought to your veterinarian's attention immediately.

In addition, it's important to have your puppy's stools tested regularly for internal parasites, as puppies are known to gnaw on sticks and put other things in their mouths that will introduce internal parasites to their systems. (See chapter 6, "Your Yorkie's Health," for more

VACCINATION SCHEDULE (6 MONTHS-ADULT)

The following vaccination schedule is recommended by the American Animal Hospital Association:

Vaccine	Age for Boosters
Distemper	1 year, then every 3 years
Parvovirus	1 year, then every 3 years
Parainfluenza	1 year, then every 3 years
Coronavirus	1 year, then every 3 years
Canine adenovirus-2	1 year, then every 3 years
Leptospirosis	1 year, then every 3 years
Bordetella *	1 year, then as needed
Lyme disease *	1 year, then prior to tick season
Rabies +	1 year, then every 3 years

* Optional vaccines, depending on location and risk.

+ Required by law. Some states still require annual boosters.

Source: American Animal Hospital Association

information on keeping your Yorkshire Terrier healthy and fit.)

SOCIALIZATION

Socialization must be an ongoing process throughout your Yorkshire Terrier's life. Although its impact on your Yorkie's psychological development is most critical during the fear development stage, which occurs between the ages of eight weeks and six months, exposing your dog to social opportunities beyond that age will continue to provide benefits for your dog.

Too many small dogs are kept like princesses in towers, confined to their homes and yards for most of their lives. It's easy to understand how this happens when you consider that small dogs don't need to leave their homes and yards to get sufficient exercise, but such confinement can make a small dog quite territorial and overprotective of his home. If he doesn't have the opportunity to

Make sure that your pampered Yorkie gets out of the house regularly. Exposing her to as many people and other animals as possible will make her a happier, less fearful dog.

meet new people and new dogs once in a while, he's not going to know how to react appropriately when he encounters them.

Training classes, dog walking, traveling, and parks all offer opportunities to get your dog out to see the world. You do need to be cognizant of your dog's small size and protect him from large dogs and boisterous children, but don't get into the habit of carrying your pup everywhere. He needs to explore the world on his own four feet.

BASIC OBEDIENCE TRAINING

Your dog is at a wonderful age for training, as his retention and attention span have improved considerably. You can enjoy training your dog to do just about anything you'd like,

but be sure to devote some time to good manners. Basic obedience commands are considered the minimum requirements for a well-behaved dog, and they are also the foundation for any other type of training discipline you may have in mind.

You may find it easier to train your Yorkie if you place him on a chair or a table, but you need to be sure your dog does not fall off and get injured. You can also sit on the floor to conduct this training. It's easier to communicate with your small dog if you're both on the same level, rather than expecting your dog to look up at you.

SIT: Sitting is such a natural position for dogs that your Yorkie will often adopt this position on his own. If you reward him with praise or treats each time he

Food rewards have become very popular in dog training, but this approach has some drawbacks. Feeding a dog too many treats can have a devastating effect on his diet, and this is even more pronounced with small dogs like Yorkshire Terriers. When using food rewards to help train your little dog, use very small treats, preferably no larger than the tip of your little finger. Also, limit your training sessions to avoid feeding your dog too many treats in one day.

"Down" and "stay" are convenient commands that will enable you to keep your Yorkie from getting into trouble.

DOWN: You can teach your dog to lie down on command by starting from the sit position. Hold a treat on the floor in front of your dog and slowly drag it away from him. This will encourage your dog to stretch out his head and front feet as he tries to keep his nose close to the treat. If your dog stretches out even a little bit, reward him with the treat. Even if your dog has not yet reached a full down position, you should reward any movement he makes in the right direction, as many obedience skills are best taught in small increments.

If your dog stands up or gets out of position, put him back into a sit and start over. A lot of patience, combined with small enough "baby steps," will eventually result in the desired behavior. Then, you can begin using the "down" command so your dog can learn to associate this word with the correct position.

STAY: The "stay" command is very useful for controlling the movement of your dog, especially in situations where safety is a concern. This command involves two components—

does it, and eventually add the "sit" command, you can teach your dog to sit at your whim. If your dog can't figure it out quite this easily, you can help him into the sit position by holding a treat above his head, just behind his eye level. When he looks up to keep his eyes on the treat, his back end may naturally drop into a sit. If not, you can further assist your dog by scooping his back legs underneath him. Plenty of repetition and generous rewards when he gets it right will have your dog sitting like an Obedience competition champ.

FAST FACT

The Yorkshire Terrier tends to score modestly on canine intelligence scales, but independent-minded terriers don't lack intelligence; they simply have less interest in obedience. Your little Yorkie will have plenty of incentive to learn just about anything you want to teach him, as long as you use positive training methods with plenty of rewards.

distance and duration—that must be taught in increments. You can work on both at the same time, provided you take this training slow and don't push your dog to progress faster than he is ready.

With your dog in a sitting position, tell him to "Stay," take one step away from him, and then step toward him immediately. If your dog has maintained his sitting position, reward him. Repeat this a couple times. When your dog remains seated consistently when you take one step away, you can advance to two steps away, and so on. Gradually increase both the distance and the duration. If your dog breaks his stay at any point, it's an indication that you're expecting too much too fast. Back up a few steps and progress more slowly.

The "stay" command will become a little more challenging for your dog

when you are ready to practice out-of-sight stays. Your dog likes to know where you are at all times, and the minute you step out of the room, he'll attempt to follow you. Set your dog up for success by stepping out of the room for only a fraction of a second in the beginning. Return immediately to reward your dog. This way, your dog will learn that you fully intend to come back, and he'll be a little more patient in waiting for longer periods of time.

COME: The "come" command is the most important skill you can teach your dog. A dog that does not come when called is an accident waiting to happen. That's why you should practice "come" every chance you get. Keep some treats in your pocket and call your dog from different rooms in your house at different times of the day. Call your dog only once each time and reward him whenever he responds. If he doesn't come on the first call, he gets no reward.

You can practice "come" outdoors in a fenced area or on a long leash, but again, only call your dog once each time and only reward your dog when he responds immediately. Don't force your dog to come to you by pulling on his leash, or he will quickly learn that "come" is only mandatory when he's on a leash. Instead, coax your dog to you by calling him in a happy voice or running a few steps away from him to encourage him to chase you.

The whole purpose of practicing the "come" command constantly is to condition your dog to respond automatically, without thinking about it, so that he will eventually listen to you even in the face of distractions. The "come" should always be presented in an upbeat manner, because if you scold or punish your dog when he doesn't come immediately, he won't be in much of a hurry to come to you the next time.

ALTERNATIVE CARE FOR YOUR YORKSHIRE TERRIER

As much as you might want to include your Yorkshire Terrier in every moment of your life, situations do arise that force you to leave your dog behind. Very few employers allow dogs in the workplace, and there are always family emergencies, business trips, and other times when

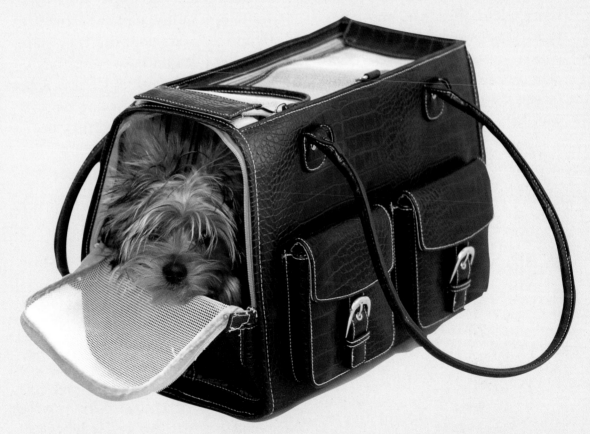

You won't always be able to take your Yorkie along—even if he will fit in a handheld pet carrier!

your dog won't be welcome to join you. Having an alternative care plan can help you get through these times without worrying about what will become of your dog.

BOARDING KENNELS: If a boarding kennel with cement floors and chain-link fencing doesn't seem like a fitting temporary residence for the little prince who occupies the softest corner of your sofa, you can check out one of the many other options in the pet boarding industry today. Boarding kennels now range from those with traditional bare-bones kennel runs to posh facilities with deluxe suites, complete with television sets and all the amenities of home. Some offer their canine guests social time with other dogs, custom cuisine, massage, aromatherapy, and professional grooming. Contact boarding facilities in your area to find out what services they offer.

Always visit a boarding kennel in person before entrusting the staff with your dog. Regardless of their accommodations, the facility should be clean and well managed by knowledgeable staff. Trust your instincts when choosing a boarding facility. No one knows what your dog needs better than you.

PET SITTERS: Pet sitters are a wonderful option if you're concerned about the stress your dog may suffer by being put into the strange environment of a boarding facility. A pet sitter can care for your dog right in your own home. A pet sitter can

Not all dog-care facilities are created equal, so check out prospective boarding kennels to make sure that they are right for your Yorkie.

offer housesitting services as well, by bringing in the newspapers and mail, watering the plants, and turning the lights on at night while you're on a vacation or a business trip.

A pet sitter can care for your Yorkie in many other situations, too. Some pet sitters offer midday dog walks and evening visits for pet owners who work long hours. This can make pet ownership much easier if you have a very demanding job or other obligations.

You should interview a pet sitter as seriously as you would a babysitter for your children. The pet sitter should be knowledgeable about dogs and show a genuine interest in your pet. You can obtain referrals for pet sitters in your area by visiting the website for the National Association of Professional Pet Sitters (NAPPS) at www.petsitters.org.

DOGGY DAY CARES: Doggy day care is a relatively new type of dog care service that allows pet owners to drop their dogs off at the start of the workday and pick them up after work, similar to a day care center for children. This is a wonderful service if you own an active dog that needs a positive outlet for his energy while you're at work. Dogs are allowed social playtime with other dogs and are also given quiet times to rest.

Like boarding facilities, doggy day cares have been evolving to include a number of different services, such as boarding, veterinary care, professional grooming, and alternative therapies. While this kind of full-service facility may be an evolving trend, you still need to carefully evaluate the doggy day care. In order to provide adequate supervision, a doggy day care should not have more than 10 dogs per staff member. It should conduct rigorous screening of the day care participants to make sure all the dogs will get along together. There should also be safeguards in place to prevent fights and accidents, and to keep dogs from escaping from the premises.

No matter how wonderful a doggy day care appears to be, there are always special concerns that apply to small dogs. Dogs love to roughhouse, and as big as your Yorkie thinks he is, he can still be injured quite easily by the rough play of larger dogs. A doggy day care would only be appropriate for your diminutive terrier if he's placed in a group with other toy dogs.

CHAPTER EIGHT

Caring for Your Adult Yorkie

The playful antics of a Yorkshire Terrier puppy are delightfully entertaining. You might dread the eventual end of your dog's puppyhood, but when your dog enters his adult phase, you'll be pleasantly surprised to discover that he has not completely lost his silly side. He'll be just as much fun, but there are some changes in him that have occurred so gradually you may not have even noticed them.

Your Yorkie may take his watchdog duties a little more seriously.

Your adult Yorkie will gladly join you on all your excursions.

You rarely have to remind him what the rules are anymore. And he seems to listen better. You wouldn't have passed up your dog's puppyhood for anything, but now you get to experience the wonderful benefits of your dog's maturity.

HEALTH CONCERNS

Your dog's immune system will have built up sufficient antibodies to protect him from most viral and bacterial diseases by now, thanks to all his vaccines. Hereditary diseases, however, are a different story. Hereditary problems can crop up at any time. Some hereditary diseases are known to affect dogs at a young age, while others can manifest symptoms at any time during a dog's life span.

The kinds of problems you should continue to watch for with your adult Yorkie include the limping associated with a luxating patella or Legg-Calves-Perthes disease, the vision loss associated with cataracts or progressive retinal atrophy, or the hair loss associated with Cushing's disease. Keep in mind that the incidence of hereditary problems can be quite low, depending on the breeding of your dog, but it doesn't hurt to be on the lookout for any symptoms. (See chapter six, "Your Yorkie's Health," for further information about these kinds of health concerns.)

NUTRITION

During his adulthood, obesity is a greater threat to your dog's health than disease. An estimated 25 to 40 percent of companion dogs in America and Great Britain are overweight. The trend toward obesity in pets appears to be mirroring the human trend toward obesity, and for the same reasons—too much food and too little exercise. You can avoid adding your dog to these dire statistics by engaging in healthy feeding practices. Limit his consumption of treats. Measure the amount of food you give him, and cut back on his rations if he seems to be developing a barrel-shaped body. Also, don't forget to provide regular, daily exercise for your dog!

EXERCISE

Exercising your dog is something that is just as good for you as it is for your Yorkie. Getting your dog outside for a daily walk is a great way to get some fresh air and moderate exercise, but it can be so much more than that. Use your walks to constantly strengthen your dog's social skills. Walking your dog will also give you opportunities to reinforce your dog's training. Insist that he walk without pulling, ask him to sit before crossing intersections, and instruct

Your Yorkie will enjoy daily walks, and the exercise will help keep him fit and healthy.

him to ignore certain distractions. All of this will help make your dog more responsive to you and strengthen your bond with him.

A good walk can help drain some of your vivacious Yorkie's energy reserves, but it doesn't do a whole lot for his cardiovascular system. That's why a good aerobic workout should also be on your dog's exercise schedule. A feisty game of fetch or a demanding game of tug will get your little guy's heart pumping. Better yet, if you and your Yorkie are so

inclined, your regular participation in Agility, Flyball, or other physically demanding dog sports will keep your dog in top condition.

ADVANCED TRAINING AND ACTIVITIES

Dog sports do not always consist of heavy physical exercise. Besides athletic-type sports, there are dog shows and Obedience trials that can satisfy your craving for competition. Not the competitive type? Then you might want to consider one of the

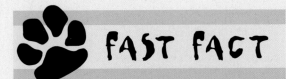

FAST FACT

Your Yorkie may be too small to run beside you, but pet accessory manufacturers have found ways around that. Pet strollers and bike carts have infiltrated the pet market, so go ahead and take your Yorkshire Terrier with you on a run. Your Yorkie would love the opportunity to get out and about for some fresh air, but don't forget to make sure he gets his own exercise!

many noncompetitive activities you can enjoy with your dog.

AGILITY: Agility is not a sport for either dogs or humans who have an aversion to physical activity. This fast-paced dog sport combines speed, agility, and obedience with an obstacle course that includes tunnels, jumps, and climbing apparatus. Even though the obstacles are intended for the dogs, the handlers have to be quick on their feet in order to direct their dogs through the course. The fastest dog through the course without penalties wins.

Your rambunctious terrier would no doubt love the challenge of Agility, because he has the energy and drive to put his heart into it. But do you have a passion for it? Sometimes, the only way to find out

is to try. A beginning Agility class at a local training facility is the best way to get started. You might just discover that the speed and adrenaline of Agility gets you just as excited as your dog! You can find more information about Agility for small dogs by visiting the Teacup Dogs Agility Association (TDAA) Web site, www.dogagility.org. You can even consider making your own equipment for backyard use. This is a sport that can be done for fun at home if you're only interested in fun and fitness.

FLYBALL: Flyball is another action-packed sport perfectly suited to a high-energy Yorkie. If your Yorkie is a ball-fetching maniac, this sport will give him his ball fix while you get to enjoy the camaraderie of being part of a team. Flyball teams consist of four dogs that each take their turn running the course in relay style.

The Flyball course is 51 feet (15.6 meters) long with four hurdles. At the end of the course sits a Flyball box that releases a ball when the dog steps on a pedal on the front of the box. Each dog is required to traverse the four hurdles, retrieve a ball from the box, and return through the course to his handler. The next dog on the team then takes his turn, and so on, until all four dogs have run the course. The team with the fastest time, minus any deductions for penalties, wins.

The jumps on a Flyball course are adjusted to fit the smallest dog on the team, so there is no need to worry that your small Yorkie can't handle it. If you want to try it out, check local training facilities for the availability of Flyball classes, or visit the North American Flyball Association (NAFA) Web site, www.flyball.org, to locate a Flyball club in your area.

CANINE MUSICAL FREESTYLE AND HEELWORK TO MUSIC: Canine Musical Freestyle is not quite as physically demanding as Agility or Flyball, but it's no less exciting and fun. A sport that combines music, colorful costumes for both dogs and handlers, tricks, and obedience,

Freestyle is one of the most entertaining of all the dog sports. Handlers and their dogs perform creative dance-type maneuvers to music, which is why it is informally called "dog dancing."

Heelwork to Music is a branch of Canine Musical Freestyle that focuses on obedience skills. A slightly more technical form of Freestyle, in Heelwork to Music dogs must perform specific skills at increasingly difficult levels of competition. The main titling authority for Canine Musical Freestyle and Heelwork to Music in the United States is the World Canine Freestyle Organization (WCFO).

Yorkshire Terriers possess more than enough intelligence and nimbleness to perform well in this sport. If your particular Yorkie loves to do tricks for treats, and you enjoy bopping to a beat, this may be a very rewarding hobby for both of you. You can find more information on this sport, or locate a local Freestyle club, by visiting the WCFO Web site, www.worldcaninefreestyle.org.

CONFORMATION: Perhaps you think you have the most gorgeous Yorkie in the world, and it's not just your pride talking. Your dog has a noble pedigree and the physical characteristics to prove it. You

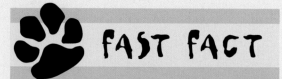

FAST FACT

Any type of training activity can help you develop a closer bond with your dog. If you don't want to make a commitment to an advanced training class, spend a little time a couple nights a week teaching your Yorkie some tricks. Your dog will love to entertain you for treats!

SHOW GROOMING

You've probably been awed by the glamorous photos of Yorkshire Terriers in full regalia, with tresses flowing to the floor and topknots dressed in perfect little bows. If you've dreamed of owning a show dog or even envisioned keeping your pet in such pristine condition, you need to know that beauty doesn't come naturally. If you ever saw a beauty queen two hours before a beauty pageant, you'd be appalled at her appearance. She certainly doesn't look anywhere near as beautiful with curlers in her hair and her face sans makeup as she does walking down the runway.

The show Yorkie, too, must endure hair wraps to protect his hair from damage and keep it from getting tangled. (Precious hairs may be broken trying to get out a single tangle.) The Yorkies you see in photos and at dog shows are just the end result of such extensive beauty practices. Their hair may be treated with color-enhancing shampoos and conditioners that give their coats just the right amount of silkiness. Their coats have been trimmed to perfection and stains have been removed or covered up with specialized products.

Which products to use and how to use them to achieve the right results are secrets of the trade that can only be learned by observing those more experienced in show grooming. The best way to learn show grooming is to find a mentor who is willing to teach you. If you're not comfortable preparing your dog for his first few shows, you can hire a professional handler who will take care of grooming and exhibiting your dog. Mentors and professional handlers can be found through your dog's breeder, a local Yorkshire Terrier club, or the Yorkshire Terrier Club of America (YTCA).

If you're a dog-show novice, you may want to hire a professional to groom your Yorkie.

know this because you have sought expert advice on choosing a show-quality dog, and now your dog is ready to start earning his royal title of champion.

There is more to showing a dog than meets the eye. You must know the Yorkshire Terrier breed standard backwards and forwards. You must become adept at the art of disguising slight Conformation flaws. You must learn how to keep your Yorkie's coat in perfect condition. You and your dog must learn the skills necessary to present yourselves in the best possible light in the show ring. Unfortunately, you must also learn the politics of the sport, which entails getting to know who is who in the dog show business. Judging is a very subjective job, and your Yorkie will invariably show better before some judges than others.

You can learn the art of Yorkie show grooming from your dog's breeder, a professional handler, or another mentor. Ring skills are best learned by taking a Conformation

Competing in a Conformation event requires a huge investment in time and money, but can be very rewarding for both you and your Yorkie. These Yorkshire Terriers are being posed for judging at the Crufts Dog Show, the largest show in the United Kingdom.

FAST FACT

One of the dog sports often overlooked by Yorkie owners is Tracking. Just because your dog has a tiny nose doesn't mean he can't follow a scent! He's just as big a hunter on the inside as those shepherds and retrievers. Just about any AKC breed can compete in Tracking, an event in which all "tests" are either pass or fail. This means you don't have to compete against other dogs. If your dog passes the appropriate test, he earns a title!

class at a local dog-training facility and then practicing your skills at a few "fun matches" offered by the AKC. And of course, much can be gained by observing the experts at work. Attend as many dog shows as you can and try to speak to exhibitors in between classes to get an inside look at this sport. (For more information, see the Show Grooming sidebar in this chapter, page 97.)

OBEDIENCE: If you gain an enormous sense of accomplishment from training your dog, Obedience competition can provide additional rewards for your efforts! Along with the benefits of having a well-trained dog, your dog can earn titles for each level of Obedience he achieves. Novice Obedience classes involve basic obedience skills, Open level classes include some off-leash work, and the Utility level, which is the crowning glory of Obedience competition, involves such impressive skills as retrieving over jumps and scent work. Obedience training classes are offered at many dog-training facilities, with advanced classes often tailored to meet the needs of the class participants.

A relatively new type of AKC Obedience competition, called Rally, involves a course consisting of 10 to 20 stations. Each station has a sign indicating the skill that needs to be completed, and handlers and their dogs work their way through the course at their own pace. Designed for the "traditional pet owner," Rally scoring is not as rigorous as an Obedience trial. You can find more information on this fun and useful sport by visiting the AKC Web site, www.akc.org.

THERAPY DOG WORK: You don't have to be involved in a competitive sport to do something worthwhile with your dog. One of the most enjoyable and noble activities you can do with your dog is to volunteer your time to improve the lives of others. Therapy dogs come in all different

Because of their cute appearance and friendly personality, Yorkshire Terriers that enjoy attention from strangers can make excellent therapy dogs.

the spirits of people in need, but that doesn't mean he's a perfect candidate for therapy dog work. Some Yorkies may be a little too excitable, some may feel uncomfortable being handled by strangers, and some may be frightened by wheelchairs or other health care equipment.

To find out which dogs have the right personality traits for therapy dog work, several organizations have designed testing and certification programs, including Therapy Dogs International (TDI) and the Delta Society. You can learn more about these organizations by checking out their Web sites, www.tdi-dog.org and www.deltasociety.org, respectively. You might also investigate the availability of training classes in your area that can help prepare your dog for certification.

Personality and training are important, but there is also the issue of size to be considered. Rough or uncoordinated handling by children, patients, or nursing home residents can cause harm to a small dog, so you must keep this in mind when choosing what type of therapy dog work to pursue. If you are willing to make the commitment, and your Yorkie has what it takes, therapy dog work can be one of the most pleasurable ways to share your dog with the world.

breeds, and they participate in all different types of programs. They provide companionship for the elderly and infirm. They give children confidence in reading. They teach the value of unconditional love to prison inmates.

Your sweet Yorkie definitely has the perky persona needed to boost

AKC Canine Good Citizen:

Even if you don't think you have the time for competitive dog sports or other activities, there is one type of advanced training every dog owner should consider. The AKC Canine Good Citizen program was designed by the AKC to encourage responsible dog ownership and to recognize dogs and their owners who have taken the extra steps to be good citizens. (A similar program is available for British dog owners through the Kennel Club of the United Kingdom.)

The program involves a 10-item test that evaluates dogs for their manners around people and other dogs. It also allows dog owners to demonstrate their responsible attitudes toward dog ownership. Dogs and their owners who pass all 10 criteria are awarded the CGC certification.

This certification program has become so well respected that many states have passed CGC resolutions that commend the AKC for this program and support the values it promotes. The CGC has also become a

FAST FACT

In order to earn an AKC CGC certificate, a dog must accept a friendly stranger, sit politely for petting, walk nicely on a leash (even through a crowd), obey basic obedience commands, and maintain his composure when confronted by other dogs, distractions, or separation from his owner. The dog's owner must demonstrate her responsible attitude toward dog ownership through the grooming and handling of her dog.

major component of therapy dog testing for TDI. It's not surprising that CGC dogs are often welcome in business establishments that normally prohibit dogs.

You can check local dog-training facilities for classes that can help prepare your dog for Canine Good Citizen testing, and you can find registered CGC evaluators listed on the AKC Web site, www.akc.org. Passing this test will entitle you to a beautiful certificate you can hang on the wall with pride.

Caring for Your Senior Yorkshire Terrier

An old dog is like an old feather bed—it's warm, comfortable, and has been contoured by age to fit you perfectly. As your dog ages, you'll realize that an old friend is the best kind of friend in the world. You'll obviously want your Yorkie to live a long and happy life, and, thanks to modern nutrition and vet-erinary care, your dog has a very good chance to do just that.

HEALTH PROBLEMS RELATED TO AGING

Aging is a very gradual process, so the signs of aging can creep up unde-tected. You may not notice signs of joint stiffness until the day your

Most Yorkies are energetic and should be able to keep up with you even as they age.

Yorkie can't jump up on the couch any more. Signs of vision loss may not be apparent until your dog actually starts bumping into things. And signs of weight gain can escape your attention until your dog's health becomes adversely affected. So try to be aware of the gradual changes in your dog, because some age-related conditions can be cured or managed to improve the quality of life for your old dog.

ARTHRITIS: When it comes to old age, stiff joints often come with the territory. You can tell if your senior Yorkie suffers from arthritis if he has difficulty getting up or lying down, jumping onto the furniture, or he moves with a stiff gait. Some dogs find relief from arthritis pain with dietary supplements that contain glucosamine and chondroitin, which help lubricate the joints.

Just like people who have arthritis, this kind of "aching in the bones" can flare up with weather conditions or periods of greater activity or exertion. For these bouts of increased pain, your veterinarian may recommend a simple pain reliever—aspirin. Check with your veterinarian for the correct dose.

You can also manage your dog's environment to avoid aggravating his condition. Stair ramps, orthopedic

Even though your Yorkie is getting older, he still requires regular exercise for optimum health. Continue taking him for his daily walk, just slow down the pace if necessary.

foam beds, heated beds, and other items are available to assist arthritic dogs. Be sure to keep your dog's bed away from drafts and avoid exposing your dog to extremes of heat and cold. Moderate exercise is a great way to keep your dog's joints flexible. Now, more than ever, it's important to monitor your dog's weight, as

ALTERNATIVE AND HOLISTIC CARE

Many veterinarians now specialize in one or more alternative therapies, which can be used in conjunction with conventional medicine to improve the quality of life for your senior Yorkshire Terrier.

Chinese Herbal Medicine: This ancient art has a very long history of success in treating a variety of illnesses and symptoms. Herbs can be just as dangerous as drugs, however, if they're not used correctly. To find a veterinarian skilled in their use, visit the Veterinary Botanical Medicine Association Web site, www.vbma.org.

Homeopathy: Homeopathy is another popular alternative treatment modality. It uses minute amounts of various disease-causing substances to treat those diseases. A list of veterinarians certified in this specialty can be found at the Academy of Veterinary Homeopathy Web site, www.theavh.org.

Acupuncture: Acupuncture, a treatment consisting of placing tiny needles into the skin at specific points to promote the free flow of "life energy" (called *chi* or *qi*), has become a very popular treatment for humans. It's now becoming widely available for animals, too. The International Veterinary Acupuncture Society certifies veterinarians in this specialty. Check out its Web site, www.ivas.org, for more information.

excess weight can put undue stress on arthritic joints.

WEIGHT GAIN OR LOSS: If you found it tricky to prevent excess weight gain in your adult Yorkie, you'll find it even trickier to keep your senior Yorkie svelte. Older dogs tend to sleep more and exercise less, which dramatically reduces the amount of calories they need to consume. With such a decrease in activity, weight gain is inevitable unless you make adjustments in your dog's diet.

If you can't seem to keep your dog's weight under control by reducing how much you feed him, a consultation with your veterinarian is in order. Your veterinarian can rule out health issues as a cause of your dog's weight gain, and can suggest an appropriate low-calorie diet, if necessary.

Weight loss is also a common problem with older dogs. A diminishing sense of taste in old dogs can cause a reduction in appetite. Dental problems may also be to blame, as they can cause pain while eating. A loss of teeth can make eating difficult for some older dogs. Weight loss can also be attributed to a number of health conditions, so any weight loss calls for a visit to your veterinarian. A change in diet or treatment of underlying health issues can help improve your dog's appetite.

DENTAL PROBLEMS: Dental problems can be the root of much misery for older small dogs. This is the phase of life when years of accumulated plaque along the gum line begin to create the most problems. Besides causing pain, loss of teeth, and difficulty eating, infections resulting from periodontal disease can travel through your dog's circulatory system to wreak havoc on internal organs. The results can be quite serious.

Give your senior Yorkie's teeth extra attention. Make sure your dog's teeth are checked regularly by a veterinarian (some veterinarians recommend twice-yearly dental checkups for senior small dogs). Your veterinarian may recommend a professional teeth cleaning, which involves anesthetizing your dog and removing all the tartar and plaque from his teeth. The cost of this procedure is well worth it, because it

FAST FACT

If you need to give your dog medication in pill form, you'll quickly realize how much dogs detest taking pills. You can take the fight out of this process by wrapping the pill in a small piece of cheese or stuffing it into a piece of hot dog. Your Yorkie will not only take the disguised pill willingly, he'll look forward to the next one!

also involves polishing the teeth so that tartar will not stick to them quite so easily in the future.

LOSS OF SENSES: Just like older people, an older dog's senses tend to wane with age. The loss of hearing and vision are so gradual that most dogs adjust quite well to the deficiencies—it's their owners who have to make concessions for them. If you notice that your dog doesn't always respond to you unless you speak loudly, you may want to use an attention-getting noise, like a loud clap or a whistle. Your dog can learn to respond to this noise as readily as if you called him by name. As long as you can get your dog's attention, you can then communicate to him what you want through hand signals and body language. Since dogs are

FAST FACT

When it comes to providing the best quality of life for your senior dog and extending his life, you need to catch any health condition early and treat it early. That's why many veterinarians now recommend twice-yearly exams for senior dogs. Your vet may also recommend an annual blood test to make sure all your dog's body systems are functioning properly.

naturally very adept at visual communication, your Yorkie will no doubt pick up on these communication signals fairly easily.

A reduction in visual acuity is also a very natural age-related physical change. The lenses of the eyes harden with age, which makes them less flexible and unable to focus. These changes result in a reduction of vision, but not total blindness. Your Yorkie can get along just fine with this deficiency, but you should remember that his vision is poorest in dim light. You must be aware of your dog's sensory deficiencies in order to prevent accidents and keep your Yorkie safe.

INCONTINENCE: People don't like to talk about incontinence. They fear that it's an inevitable consequence of old age, which cannot be managed or cured, but this isn't always true. Many cases of incontinence are caused by a loss of muscle tone in the sphincter muscle, which normally keeps urine from escaping from the bladder. When this muscle relaxes too much, a dog may leak urine while he's sleeping, or he may have trouble "holding it" as long as he used to. Medication has been shown to help with this problem, so ask your veterinarian about treatment.

Other health conditions, such as a reduction in kidney function, may also cause incontinence. These, too, can sometimes be managed with medication or dietary changes, so seek your veterinarian's advice. In addition, you can manage incontinence by giving your older

FAST FACT

Strange behavior in your senior Yorkie, such as getting lost in the house, forgetting his housetraining, or acting out of character could be a sign of canine cognitive dysfunction, which is similar to Alzheimer's disease in humans. A healthy lifestyle that includes nutritious food and regular exercise will help preserve your Yorkie's mental health well into his old age.

Even though he's slowing down, your senior Yorkie can still be a lot of fun!

dog plenty of potty breaks and providing him with washable bedding that can be easily cleaned, when necessary.

FAILING ORGANS: Other body parts that tend to become less efficient with age include the heart, the stomach, and the kidneys. If your dog just doesn't seem to have much energy or has difficulty recovering from exercise, he may be suffering from some degree of heart failure. If your dog consumes an excessive amount of water and tends to urinate a lot, his liver and kidneys may not be operating efficiently. And if he refuses to eat and vomits occasionally, he may have developed a sensitive stomach.

All these issues can be managed or treated with the help of your veterinarian, so make note of any symptoms and bring them to your veterinarian's attention. Getting old is inevitable, but you can often alleviate the symptoms of old age for your senior Yorkie. Your old friend deserves the best quality of life you can provide.

Medication, combined with regular exercise and proper nutrition, can delay or ease the symptoms of aging in your Yorkshire Terrier.

CANCER: The six-letter word that strikes fear into anyone who hears it isn't as ominous as it once was. Cancer still suffers from the terminal reputation it developed in the past, despite the many medical advances that have been made in cancer detection and treatment over the years. Some forms of cancer now offer very good prognoses, even for dogs.

Since cancer presents itself in so many different forms and degrees of severity, the symptoms vary greatly. Of particular concern would be any unusual growths, lumps, or behaviors, which should be brought to your veterinarian's attention immediately. Regardless of the type of cancer, early detection and early treatment yield the best results.

EXERCISE

Your saucy terrier may act like a perennial pup even when old age tries to slow him down. Many Yorkies remain young at heart well into the twilight of their lives. But no matter how much energy your Yorkie carries with him into his retirement years, his age does make him more prone to soreness and injuries. Moderate daily exercise should be on his agenda, but avoid overexerting your aged dog.

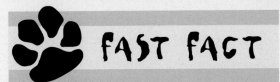

FAST FACT

Due to better diets, better living conditions, and advances in veterinary medicine, dogs are living longer than ever. Pet-product manufacturers are paying attention to the aging pet population. Supplements, special diets, low-calorie treats, and an abundance of health products and comfort devices for aging pets are now widely available at pet supply outlets.

SAYING GOOD-BYE

At some point, the day will come when your little one will pass on. It's not easy to say good-bye to such a special friend. If you're lucky, he'll pass away peacefully in his sleep, but death is rarely so serene. Chances are that you will have to decide whether or not to ease your dog's suffering at the end and help him pass from this life. Your dog may let you know when the time is right. If you look into your dog's eyes and see them squinting from the constant pain of a failing body, or you notice that they have lost the luster of life and hope, he may be telling you that life has become too great a burden.

Euthanasia is a term that means "good death." When your dog is on the last thread of life, euthanasia may be the kindest parting gift you can give your dog. Your veterinarian will inject your dog with a cocktail of drugs that will put him painlessly to sleep. Within a couple minutes, your dog's heart will stop beating and he will be at rest. It is an amazingly quiet, uneventful experience.

How you decide to deal with your dog's remains is an entirely personal decision. You can decide to have your dog cremated and even keep his ashes in an urn for remembrance. Or you can choose to have your dog's

remains buried in some fashion. Whichever you choose, it should help you find some sense of closure.

Everyone needs to cope with grief in his or her own way, and that's why it's important that you not consider what others will think of you or your actions at this difficult time. If you believe others will ridicule you because you need to take some time off work to grieve, you might be surprised to find that some of your coworkers have suffered similar

Photos of you and your pet that remind you of the good times you've shared over the years can help ease the pain of his passing.

FAST FACT

You might be surprised by the powerful emotions that grip you at the loss of your darling Yorkie. Humans have just recently begun to recognize the depth of the human-dog relationship and how profoundly the death of a cherished pet affects us. Animal shelters, social organizations, and grief counselors now offer support services for grieving pet owners, so you don't have to face the grief alone.

losses and that they understand completely. Don't let the "It's only a dog" mentality deny you the opportunity to heal from this loss.

One of the ways that can help you find closure is to memorialize your dog. Plant a tree in honor of your pet. Make a photo collage of your dog. Make a garden stone with your dog's name on it. Family participation in constructing a memorial can bring everyone a little closer and will especially help children deal with the finality of death.

Turning your loss into something positive can help remind you of the positive aspects of your life with your Yorkie. You can make a donation in your Yorkie's memory to an animal shelter, a rescue group, or another animal welfare organization. This doesn't have to be a monetary donation. You can offer your time as a volunteer. Sometimes keeping busy is the best way to keep the blues away.

Most importantly, don't forget to love. Focus on the people and pets that still grace your life. Their love will help to heal the hole in your heart. Someday, the pain will fade and only cherished memories will be left. Then, when you're ready, you might consider making new memories with a new dog.

Every phase of your dog's life provides its own treasures, so enjoy each precious day with your Yorkie. As Roger Caras, a leading authority on pets and their care, once stated so eloquently, "Dogs are not our whole lives, but they make our lives whole."

Organizations to Contact

**American Animal
Hospital Association**
12575 West Bayaud Ave.
Lakewood, CO 80228
Phone: 303-986-2800
Fax: 800-252-2242
Email: info@aahanet.org
Web site: www.aahanet.org

American Kennel Club
260 Madison Ave
New York, NY 10016
Phone: 212-696-8200
Web site: www.akc.org

Association of Pet Dog Trainers
150 Executive Center Drive, Box 35
Greenville, SC 29615
Phone: 1-800-738-3647
Fax: 1-864-331-0767
Email: information@apdt.com
Web site: www.apdt.com

The Canadian Kennel Club
89 Skyway Avenue, Suite 100
Etobicoke, Ontario
M9W 6R4 Canada
Phone: 416-675-5511
Fax: 416-675-6506
Email: information@ckc.ca
Web site: www.ckc.ca/en/

Delta Society
875 124th Avenue NE, Suite 101
Bellevue, WA 98005
Phone: 425-226-7357
Fax: 425-679-5539
Email: info@deltasociety.org
Web site: www.deltasociety.org

**The Kennel Club
of the United Kingdom**
1-5 Clarges Street
Piccadilly
London W1J 8AB
United Kingdom
Phone: 0870 606 6750
Fax: 020 7518 1058
Web site: www.thekennelclub.org.uk/

**National Association of Dog
Obedience Instructors**
PMB 369
729 Grapevine Hwy
Hurst, TX 76054-2085
Email: corrsec2@nadoi.org
Web site: www.nadoi.org

**National Association of
Professional Pet Sitters**
17000 Commerce Parkway, Suite C
Mt. Laurel, NJ 08054
Phone: 856-439-0324

Fax: 856-439-0525
Email: napps@ahint.com
Web site: www.petsitters.org

**North American Dog Agility
Council (NADAC)**
11522 South Highway 3
Cataldo, ID 83810
Email: info@nadac.com
Web site: www.nadac.com

**North American Flyball
Association (NAFA)**
1400 West Devon Avenue, #512
Chicago, IL 60660
Phone: 800-318-6312
Fax: same as phone
Email: flyball@flyball.org
Web site: www.flyball.org

Pet Sitters International
418 East King Street
King, NC 27021-9163
Phone: 336-983-9222
Fax: 336-983-3755
Web site: www.petsit.com

**Teacup Dogs Agility Association
(TDAA)**
P.O. Box 158
Maroa, IL 61756
Phone: 217-521-7955
Email: agilitygo1@msn.com
Web site: www.k9tdaa.com

Therapy Dogs International, Inc.
88 Bartley Road
Flanders, NJ 07836
Phone: 973-252-9800
Fax: 973-252-7171
Email: tdi@gti.net
Web site: www.tdi-dog.org

UK National Pet Register
74 North Albert Street, Dept 2
Fleetwood, Lancashire
FY7 6BJ
United Kingdom
Web site: www.nationalpetregister.org

**United States Dog Agility
Association, Inc. (USDAA)**
P.O. Box 850955
Richardson, TX 75085-0955
Phone: 972-487-2200
Fax: 972-272-4404
Email: info@usdaa.com
Web site: www.usdaa.com

**Yorkshire Terrier Club of America
(YTCA)**
Shirley Patterson, Secretary
P.O. Box 265
Saint Peters, PA 19470-0265
Web site: www.ytca.org

Further Reading

Arden, Darlene. *Small Dogs, Big Hearts: A Guide to Caring for Your Little Dog*. Rev. ed. New York: Howell Book House, 2006.

Coren, Stanley. *The Intelligence of Dogs: Canine Consciousness and Capabilities*. New York: Free Press, 1994.

Eldredge, Debra. *Dog Owner's Veterinary Handbook*. New York: Howell Book House, 2007.

John, Meredith, and Carole L. Richards. *Raising a Champion: A Beginner's Guide to Showing Dogs*. Collingswood, N.J.: The Well Trained Dog, 2001.

Lane, Marion. *Yorkshire Terrier: Your Happy Healthy Pet*. New York: Howell Book House, 2005.

Wood, Deborah. *Little Dogs: Training Your Pint-Sized Companion*. Neptune City, N.J.: TFH Publications, 2004.

Wood, Deborah. *The Little Dogs' Beauty Book*. Neptune City, N.J.: TFH Publications, 2006.

Internet Resources

www.aspca.org/apcc

The ASPCA Animal Poison Control Center provides lifesaving information for pet owners. The Center also has a hotline available for emergencies: 888-426-4435.

www.avma.org

The Web site of the American Veterinary Medical Association provides a wealth of information on canine health and welfare issues for pet owners.

www.canismajor.com/dog/

This Web site has a tremendous library of articles about dogs, covering everything from hereditary health issues to breed profiles. Have a question about dogs? You can look it up here.

www.petfinder.com

This site maintains a nationwide database of adoptable pets, and also provides listings of shelters and Yorkshire Terrier rescue groups.

www.petrix.com/dognames/

Can't think of a catchy name for your Yorkie? This Web site will give you all kinds of ideas, from traditional to strangely unique!

Publisher's Note: The Web sites listed on these pages were active at the time of publication. The publisher is not responsible for Web sites that have changed their address or discontinued operation since the date of publication.

Index

first-aid supplies, 69
fleas, 69–70
    See also parasites
Flyball, 95–96
    See also dog shows
food. *See* nutrition

gender differences, 37–38
Giese, Jeanna, 77
grooming, 25, 57–60, 97

Halifax Terrier. *See* Yorkshire Terriers
health issues, 43, 66–69, 83–85, 93
    dental care, 61–62, 84, 105
    and diseases, 43, 70, 71, 73–77
    ear care, 60–61
    hereditary, 43, 77–79, 84, 93
    parasites, 43, 69–73, 76, 84
    and senior dogs, 102–109
    See also Yorkshire Terriers
heartworms, 69, 71–73
    See also parasites
Heelwork to Music, 96
    See also dog shows
hepatic porto systemic shunt, 79
hereditary health problems, 43, 77–79, 84, 93
    See also health issues
holistic health care, 104
home puppy-proofing, 49–50
household rules, 50–51
housetraining, 55, 62, 64–65
    See also training
Huddersfield Ben (foundation sire), 20–21, 22, 23
Humane Society of the United States, 30, 32
hydrocephalus, 79
hypoplasia of dens, 79
hypothyroidism, 79

identification, 29–30
    See also ownership, dog
incontinence, 106, 108

independence, 10–11
    See also personality
Industrial Revolution, 9, 11, 17–18
infectious canine hepatitis, 74–75
intelligence, 88
The Intelligence of Dogs (Coren), 14, 40

jobs, 14–15, 92–93, 99–100

Kennel Club (KC), 22, 24, 101
kennel cough (bordetella), 75
keratitis sicca, 79
Kershaw's Old Kitty (dam), 20

leash laws, 33–34
legal issues, 33–35
    See also ownership, dog
Legg-Calve-Perthes disease, 43, 78, 93
leptospirosis, 75–76
liability, 35
licensing, 30
    See also ownership, dog
loss of senses, 105–106
Lyme disease, 70, 71, 76

Maltese, 20
Manchester Terrier, 19–20
microchips, 29–30
Mozart (son of Huddersfield Ben), 21

nail care, 60
National Association of Professional Pet Sitters (NAPPS), 81
National Council on Pet Population Study and Policy, 33
National Institutes of Health, 43
neutering, 30–33, 38
North American Flyball Association (NAFA), 96
nuisance laws, 34–35
nutrition, 54–56, 82–83, 93

Obedience competition, 99
    See also dog shows

Contributors

JANICE BINIOK has written numerous articles and several books on companion animals, including *The Poodle* in the OUR BEST FRIENDS series. She holds an English degree from the University of Wisconsin–Milwaukee and is a member of the Dog Writers Association of America. Janice is a former professional dog groomer, and Yorkies have been some of her best friends and clients. Janice lives on a small farm in Waukesha, Wisconsin, with her husband, two sons, and several four-legged members of the family.

Senior Consulting Editor **GARY KORSGAARD, DVM,** has had a long and distinguished career in veterinary medicine. After graduating from The Ohio State University's College of Veterinary Medicine in 1963, he spent two years as a captain in the Veterinary Corps of the U.S. Army. During that time he attended the Walter Reed Army Institute of Research and became Chief of the Veterinary Division for the Sixth Army Medical Laboratory at the Presidio, San Francisco.

In 1968 Dr. Korsgaard founded the Monte Vista Veterinary Hospital in Concord, California, where he practiced for 32 years as a small animal veterinarian. He is a past president of the Contra Costa Veterinary Association, and was one of the founding members of the Contra Costa Veterinary Emergency Clinic, serving as president and board member of that hospital for nearly 30 years.

Dr. Korsgaard retired in 2000, and currently enjoys golf, hiking, international travel, and spending time with his wife Susan and their three children and four grandchildren.